Napkin Folding
for Every Occasion

Doris Kuhn

Napkin Folding
for *Every Occasion*

Sterling Publishing Co., Inc.
New York

Photos: Frank Schuppelius
Editor: Rodman Pilgrim Neumann

Library of Congress Cataloging-in-Publication Data
Kuhn, Doris.
  Napkin folding for every occasion / Doris Kuhn.
    p. cm.
  Includes index.
  ISBN 1-4027-1012-7
  1. Napkin folding. I. Title.
TX879 .K85 2004
642'.79—dc22

                                          2003023434

        2 4 6 8 10 9 7 5 3 1

     Published 2004 by Sterling Publishing Co., Inc.
        387 Park Avenue South, New York, NY 10016
Originally published and © 2000/2002 by Englisch Verlag GmbH, Wiesbaden
          Under the titles *Servietten falten: Neue Ideen*
      and *Servietten falten: Dekorative Ideen für den Tisch*
    English Translation © 2004 by Sterling Publishing Co., Inc.
          Distributed in Canada by Sterling Publishing
      ℅ Canadian Manda Group, One Atlantic Avenue, Suite 105
             Toronto, Ontario, Canada M6K 3E7
      Distributed in Great Britain by Chrysalis Books Group PLC,
    The Chrysalis Building, Bramley Road, London W10 6 SP, England.
    Distributed in Australia by Capricorn Link (Australia) Pty. Ltd.
          P.O. Box 704, Windsor, NSW 2756, Australia

          Sterling ISBN 1-4027-1012-7

Contents

Preface

A lovingly set table can make any occasion special and always sets the tone for the meal to come. A festive dinner table is almost unthinkable without stylishly folded napkins to add the perfect finishing touch. It is no accident that fine restaurants have long preserved the art of napkin folding as an important element of presentation.

A well-cared-for table is especially appreciated today, not only in restaurants, but also in the private sphere, for less formal occasions such as a family dinner, a meal with friends, a chat over coffee, or even a colorful children's birthday party. Napkins are the finsihing detail of a successful table decoration time and again. Whether for a large gala dinner party or for a romantic meal for two, with the right know-how ordinary napkins turn into extraordinary decorative elements, adding an elegant touch that will delight your guests.

The napkin has, in the course of its centuries-long history, taken a special place among table decorations. A rich tradition of the art of napkin folding has evolved. Nowadays, napkins are not only an integral part of our table culture as practical objects, but also as creative and imaginative decorative elements.

Since the Middle Ages, napkins have been used in courtly and cultural circles. With the arrival of chivalry, more refined table manners also made their arrival in Europe. It soon became unseemly to drink out of a cup or goblet with greasy lips or to wipe one's hands on the tablecloth.

So, with time, these newfangled "mouth-cloths" were appreciated, but, beyond their immediate practical uses, napkins did not play a major role at courtly tables.

In time, as clothes became more extravagant and costly, it occurred to people to tie napkins around their necks in order to protect their clothes. The fashionable flamboyances of this epoch resulted in the use of the napkin as a stylish cultured accessory in even the highest circles.

Under Louis XIV (1643-1715), the Sun King, known for his dissolute luxurious life, splendor knew no bounds. At his legendary banquets, each dish was presented as an ultimate feast for the eyes. For such an occasion, the table decoration had to contribute both artistically and luxuriously to a splendid stage for the feast. In the course of this development of splendor, people came up with the idea to not simply put napkins on a plate but rather to present them as small works of art by folding them into three-dimensional figures. The art of napkin folding was born as people tried to outdo each other in ever more elaborate, exuberant, and imaginative creations.

At this point, whoever thought highly of himself or herself tried to imitate the banquets of the king, and so the fashion of folding napkins into figures made its arrival among the lower nobility and even among the bourgeoisie.

After this brief look into the history of napkins, you will now understand why there is so much talk in this book about the "art of napkin folding" and why many of the figures presented come from a rich tradition. Quite a few of the napkin forms that we use were already around at the time of Louis XIV.

Perhaps you are a newcomer to the art of napkin folding, up until now only admiring from afar the distinctive napkin forms seen in restaurants, but are ready to turn such beautiful ideas into artistic accents for your own table. Perhaps you are already an accomplished "fold artist" in search of some new, unusual folding ideas. In either case, let this book inspire you with new table decorating ideas. This book offers something for everyone—simple and uncomplicated figures for everyday use, original folding suggestions for special events, new and stunning decorative ideas, as well as examples of the high art of napkin folding for really special occasions.

Detailed descriptions and drawings help the novice or experienced napkin folding artist to put even the most complicated napkin shapes into action. The folding instructions and clear drawings will show you step by step how these lovely creations can come about. Whether you wish to place some attractive accents on your table with a simple figure or, perhaps, to try an unusual creation for a special occasion, this book will inspire you.

Whether you prefer fine napkins made of fabric or practical paper napkins for your daily use, here you will find a superb napkin figure for every occasion and taste. You can refer to the illustrated index at the end of the book to select the best napkin fold for any occasion. Choose the design you want by looking at the finished result and then turning to the corresponding page for the description and folding instructions.

I wish you great joy in choosing and folding! I hope you will have fun making and using these napkin creations.

— Doris Kuhn

Napkin Folding Designs

Elegant Flower

To make the decorative Elegant Flower form, it is best to use napkins about 16 by 16 inches in size or larger. Your choice of material does not play a major role with this shape—you may use napkins made from cotton, linen, or even paper. However, the material should not be too thick, so that you can put the finished flower in a napkin ring or a narrow glass to give it the necessary support.

Folding Instructions

1. Begin with the napkin spread out face down on the table in front of you so that it stands on its tip, in the shape of a diamond. Then bring the bottom corner over the top, folding the napkin up in half into a triangle.

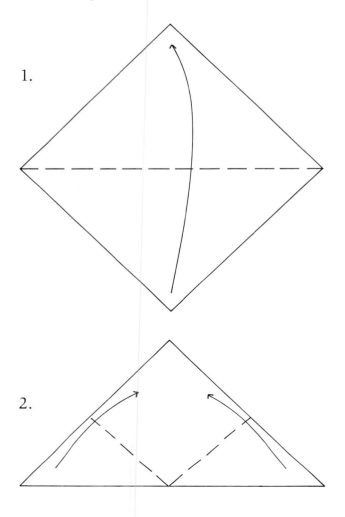

2. Now hold your finger at the center of the bottom edge as you fold up the left and right corners so that they are at the same height as, but slightly to the sides of, the top corner point.

3. The napkin should look as shown in drawing 3. In the next step, turn the napkin over so that the folded corners are underneath.

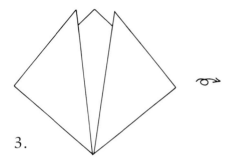

3.

4. Now fold the lower part of the napkin about one-third of the way up.

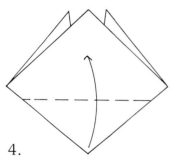

4.

5. Next, accordion-pleat the napkin in wide folds from one side across to the opposite side. Accordion pleating is a time-honored technique, also called "fanning," which means that the napkin is folded back and forth in narrow, sharp zigzag folds. In drawing 5, the dashed lines are edges where either side folds back, and the dotted lines are edges where the sides fold up. In order to create a so-called "mountain fold," that is, a fold whose edge stands up with either side folded back, running exactly through the middle, start by folding the napkin in the middle and then accordion-pleat the sides in generous folds. For this, simply fold the sides back, forth, back, and so on.

Let the folded edges should remain somewhat rounded; the edges should not be smoothed down. The Elegant Flower is best expressed through a flowing, soft movement of material rather than using very sharp edges.

6. Place the base of the napkin in a napkin ring or glass for support. Spread out the sides to shape the petals of the finished Elegant Flower.

5.

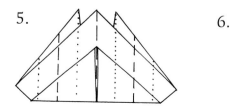

6.

Lying Lily

The mystery of the sophisticated Lying Lily with its flowing lines and elegant drapery lies in the somewhat different preparation of this napkin shape. It is not so much folded as it is created with loose creases placed into soft folds. For materials, fine paper or stiffer fabric would not be the right choice. These materials cannot be draped so softly and luxuriously. An elegant napkin figure, such as this, works best with fine fabrics like damask or linen for formal occasions. In order for your Lily not to turn out too large and so lose its contours or drape over the edge of the plate, you should not use napkins that are too large. A size of about 12 by 12 inches is ideal.

Folding Instructions

1. Spread out the napkin face down on the table in the shape of a diamond. Fold the napkin in half diagonally, bringing the bottom corner over the top corner so that the long side is at the bottom. Remember that the bottom fold is not smoothed down so that the edge forms a soft line.

2. Fold the right and left corners loosely to the back, under the napkin, so that they meet at the center point of the lower edge.

3. Loosely fold the new lower right and left corners up diagonally to form a point at the bottom. The creased corners are now resting on the surface of the napkin. Again, it is very important that that the edges are not smoothed down; the fabric is simply gently folded during the individual steps.

4. Now gather the bottom of the napkin together. By doing so, the smooth middle part of the napkin should be put into two deep, diagonal folds, the fold edges of which should now end with the two creased corners that are now turned inside out.

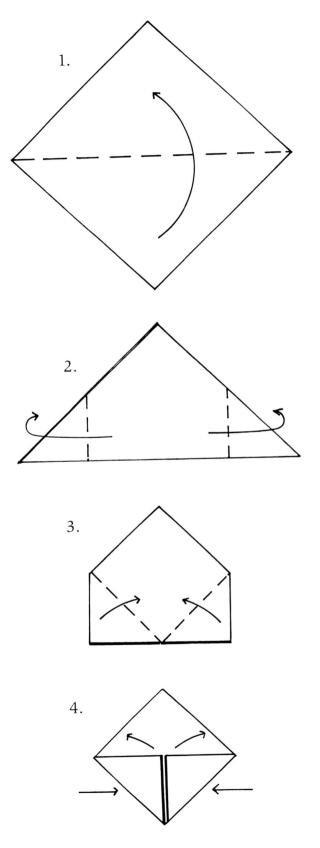

5. Place a napkin ring around the bunched end in order to hold the napkin together. Now drape the Lily over the plate. To give the Lily its finishing touch, take hold of the open right and left ends of the napkin and give these openings a slightly rounded shape.

5.

Slide

If you expect your guests to be arriving soon, or there is simply no time for lavish table decorations, quick, attractive napkin figures are called for, such as this sweeping Slide. A napkin of about 12 by 12 inches of any material, cloth or paper, is suitable, since the folding gives the figure its stability. If you are using paper napkins, the first part of step one is already done. This makes the figure even simpler, and in no time at all, you can create this beautiful and sturdy napkin form.

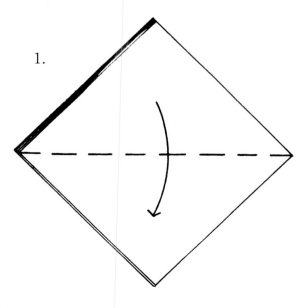

Folding Instructions

1. The starting form is a napkin folded into quarters with the loose corners at the upper right. To fold a napkin into quarters, begin with a spread out napkin in front of you. Fold the napkin in half up into a rectangle, and then crossways in half, left over right, into a square. The loose four corners will be in the upper right.

Now rotate the square in front of you counter-clockwise to a diamond standing on its tip with the loose four corners pointing up. Afterward fold the napkin in half down, as shown in drawing 1, so that you have a triangle with the point at the bottom.

2. Now fold the lower portion of the top layer of the napkin triangle once again up, folding about ¾ of an inch below the upper edge. Smooth down the crease well.

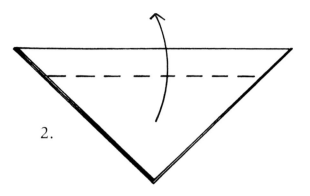

3. Then fold the napkin along an imaginary vertical centerline to the back. The crease of the fold must be smoothed down well once again.

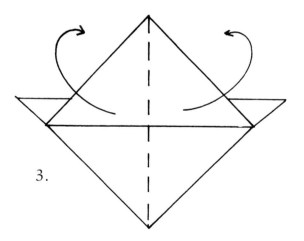

4. Set the napkin up by slightly opening the lower edges as if they now formed the sides of a triangle.

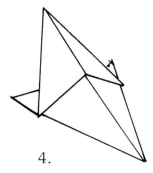

Ruffled Heart

The Ruffled Heart works very well with red or pink solid-colored napkins of about 12 by 12 inches. Heart figures that are made from fine fabric or paper become especially airy. If paper napkins are used, they should be colored on all sides. Patterned paper napkins often have a white reverse side, which would show as a fanned layer of paper.

Folding Instructions

1. Begin with an open napkin. Fold in the middle, bringing the top edge down to the bottom edge and then fold once crossways again into a square. Paper napkins are already folded in this manner. In this case, the four loose corners are at the lower right. Now rotate the napkin in front of you, so that the four loose corners point up.

2. Then fold the corner of the very top layer of the fabric or paper down onto the lower corner, by folding it down in half.

3. The second layer is folded down somewhat higher, with a distance of about ⅜ of an inch from the first edge of the fold. Thus, this tip comes to lie a little higher than the first one.

4. Fold the third layer down in the same manner, again about ⅜ of an inch higher. The folded tips and the side edges should lie at equal distance from one another.

5. Fold the last layer of the napkin down in the same manner.

6. Fold the sides of the napkin from the center point of the upper edge diagonally inward toward an imaginary centerline.

7. Then fold the tip, which rests on the very top of the napkin, horizontally to the back.

8. Unfold the smooth edges of the napkin carefully up and out. To do this, firmly hold the upper center with the creased tip, which is now on the back. The napkin should only unfold its sides.

9. To finish the last detail of the Ruffled Heart, slightly press from behind along the diagonal edges of the fold near the top. In this way, the Ruffled Heart receives a soft, curved contour.

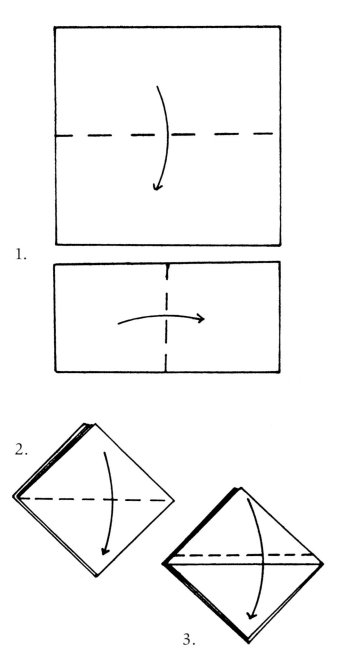

4.

5.

6.

7.

8.

9.

Cone

Through its folded tip, which springs open, this napkin figure actually has the typical shield form, but it is nevertheless called a Cone. It is this tip that catches the eye and turns this form from a simple shape into a classic design. The Cone is the perfect napkin shape to highlight pretty corner motifs such as broken lace, an embroidered monogram, or borders on your napkins. The Cone is a natural solution to attractively shaping single-colored cloth napkins or patterned fleece and paper napkins of a size of about 12 by 12 inches.

Folding Instructions

1. Spread out the napkin face down on the table in the shape of a diamond. If the napkin you are using has a corner motif or a monogram, it should lie beneath the top corner. Fold the napkin in half diagonally so that the long side is at the bottom.

2. Fold the left and right corners of the triangle, starting diagonally from the center point of the lower edge, diagonally up so that the corners meet on the upper tip.

3. The napkin should look like drawing 3. Turn the napkin over.

4. Fold the lower tip up along a fold line about 3 inches wide.

5. The sides of the napkin are now folded backward so that the napkin tapers wider from the bottom to the outside corners.

6. Now you have the finished Cone.

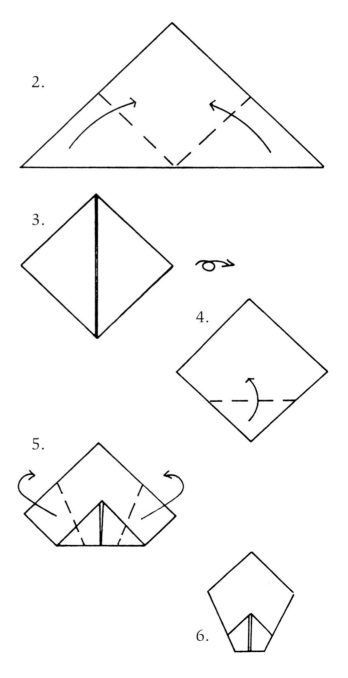

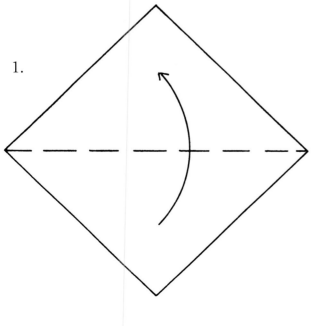

Simple Arrow

The Simple Arrow is expressed here in a clear graphic form. We are dealing with a figure whose emphasis lies in its straightness and simplicity. Thus playful napkins with flower prints or edges of lace are not quite right for this figure—rather use single-colored or simple bordered napkins in bright, deep colors. Colorful edges or borders especially accentuate the design of the Simple Arrow, since, as the napkin is folded, the border will run precisely along the edge of the shaft and arrowhead, as seen in the photo on the opposite page.

The Simple Arrow can be folded, without much effort, from 12 by 12 inch paper napkins. The open pocket at the head of the Simple Arrow is very well suited, by the way, for holding table cards or silverware. A lovely way to complement the tight simplicity of this form is by tucking a flower in the pocket.

Folding Instructions

1. Spread out the napkin face down on the table. Thus the patterned side should be underneath. Now fold the napkin in half bringing the right side over the left into a rectangle.

2. Fold the right lower corner diagonally up to the center point of the left edge.

3. Now, fold the left lower corner diagonally up onto the lower edge of the right side.

4. The two sides are now folded back to give the Simple Arrow its slim shape.

5. Arrange the finished Simple Arrow on your plate to your taste, either straight up and down or at an angle.

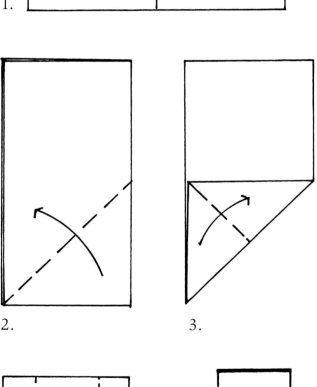

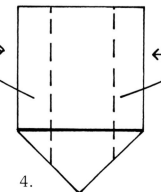

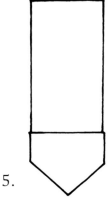

Square Knot

This design originated in the United States. Napkins folded in the Square Knot were placed on plates as well as used as coasters for bottles or glasses, because of their flat forms. The folding technique, however, is reminiscent of origami, the Japanese art of paper folding. In any case, it is an unusual, yet quite attractive addition to the art of napkin folding.

A striped napkin, as in the photo opposite, helps emphasize the interesting appearance of this form; however, a plain colored material can also look great in this shape. One more thing needs to be said regarding the material: it should not be too thick. Paper or standard cloth napkins are very well suited. If you want to use this napkin figure as a coaster, you should definitely use paper napkins so that the finished Square Knot turns out very flat with no thick seams hidden inside that might tip glasses or bottles.

Folding Instructions

1. Spread out the napkin face down on the table. Fold the upper-edge about one-fifth down and fold the lower edge about one-fifth up.

2. The napkin should now look like drawing 2. The widths of the upper and lower pieces, as well as the smooth middle piece, will each make up one third of the new height. Now first fold the lower third of the napkin up and then fold the upper third down on top of the other fold.

3. The napkin should now rest in front of you as a narrow band as shown in drawing 3. Now fold the right side, starting from the center point of the upper edge, diagonally forward; bring the former upper edge so it lies vertically across the original center of the napkin. The left side is then also folded diagonally, but this time it is folded back so that it comes to lay underneath.

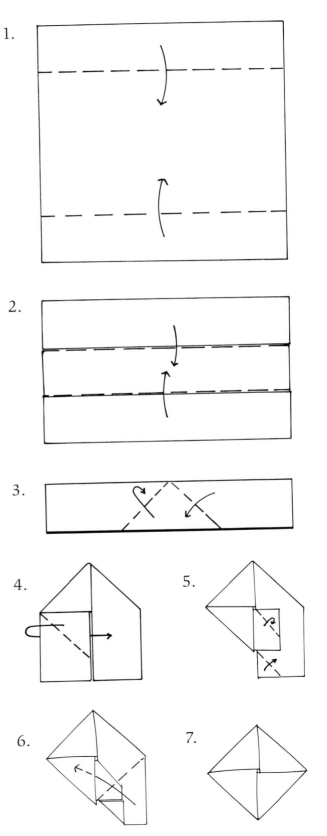

4. The end of the band, which juts out from under the left side of the napkin, is now folded, starting from the left corner, diagonally back to leave a triangle facing front. The extra length of the free end that was just folded behind is placed above the band of the right side.

5. The upper corner of the extra length that sits on top of the right half is now once again folded back and the left lower corner of the right band is now folded up.

6. At this point, the right lower corner of the right band is likewise folded diagonally up; this is done in a straight line from the upper right to the lower corner of the napkin. In doing so, the corner of the fold is slid under the neighboring triangle. The object is to get a squared figure.

7. The finished Square Knot is now placed over a plate or set out as a coaster.

Bishop's Miter

As the name suggests, this form comes from a long tradition. The elegant Bishop's Miter is one of the most popular, suitable for formal dinner invitations or great festivities. Traditional napkin forms require a large, lush napkin that holds starch well. Thus, for the Bishop's Miter, you should use cloth napkins at least 16 by 16 inches in size. Paper napkins are a possible alternative only if they are single-colored throughout. I personally believe, however, that classic figures have the greatest effect when folded with traditional materials.

Folding Instructions

1. Turn the spread-out napkin to a diamond shape on its tip in front of you. Now fold the lower part of the napkin up just below an imaginary halfway line. The edges of the top layer should be about 1 inch to 1¼ inches in from the outer edges of the layer below.

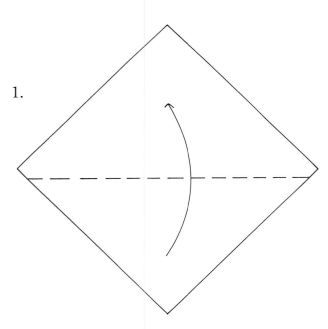

2. Now fold the two sides, each about ¾ inch from the center point of the lower edge, diagonally up so that the creased lower edges run vertically, parallel to an imaginary centerline but with a distance of about 1½ inches between them. The outside edges lie precisely on top of the edges below.

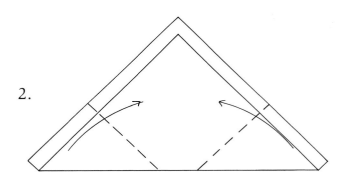

3. Then fold up the lower part of the napkin, as shown in drawing 3, along a line slightly below the outside corners.

4. This flap is now once again folded down in half.

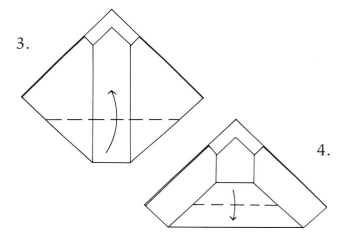

5. Finally, the sides are bent backward and the ends tucked into one another.

6. The Bishop's Miter is quite stable and can be set upright on the plate.

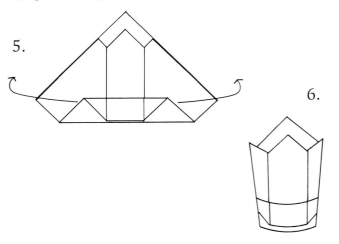

Middle Band, Diagonal Band & Diagonal Fold

The Middle Band, the Diagonal Band, and the Diagonal Fold are three classic napkin forms of simple elegance.

As these three napkin forms are created from the same basic starting shape, we will introduce them together. Even though the steps of folding are quite similar, each of these napkin creations has its own character and unmistakable charm.

The Middle Band is just right for accentuating a beautiful tablecloth. Whether for a grand dinner or a quiet foldfast table, it brings a touch of sheer elegance. The Diagonal Band, created with almost the same technique, has an entirely different appearance because of the angled run across the center. It offers a nice contrast to the rectangular shape of the form. With the Diagonal Fold, as the name indicates, a diagonally running fold lends a casual flair to soften the otherwise formal look of the flat napkin.

Basic Shape — the first steps are the same for all three variations:

1. Spread out the napkin face down on the table in front of you as a square. Thus, the patterned side should be underneath. Fold the upper fourth of the napkin down and the lower fourth up horizontally so that the top and bottom edges meet at the center.

1.

2. Now fold the lower half of the napkin up—bring the lower edge onto the upper edge. The napkin should now lie in front of you as a narrow band.

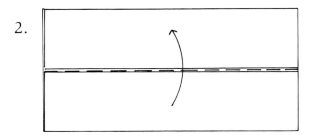

2.

Middle Band

3. In the next step, fold the very top layer of cloth, starting from the upper edge, one-third down so that this fold runs like a narrow band across the napkin.

4. Now fold the sides back, bending at an imaginary line just between a quarter to a third of the width, and tuck the ends into one another at the back.

5. The finished Middle Band can now be arranged on your plate.

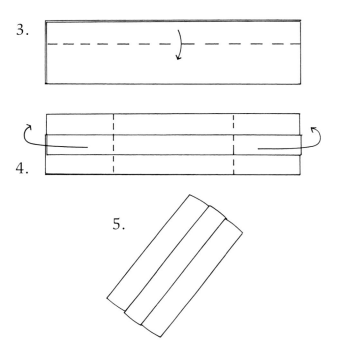

3.

4.

5.

Diagonal Band

1. + 2. Fold the Basic Shape as with the Middle Band. If you are using striped napkins, the stripes should run from left to right.

3a. Starting at the upper right corner, fold down the very top layer of cloth along an imaginary diagonal line that runs from the lower right corner to a point about one third of the top edge's width in from the top left corner.

4a. Now fold back the tip that juts below the lower edge of the napkin so that the lower edge runs straight across again.

5a. Now fold the sides back, bending at an imaginary line just between a quarter to a third of the width, and tuck the ends into one another at the back.

6a. You can now place the finished Diagonal Band on your plate.

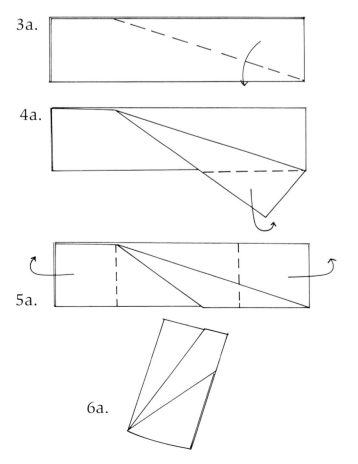

3a.

4a.

5a.

6a.

Diagonal Fold

1. + 2. Fold the Basic Shape to start with.

3b. Starting at the upper right corner, loosely fold down the very top layer of cloth along an imaginary diagonal line that runs from the lower right corner to the center point of the top edge.

4b. All that is left to do now is to fold the smooth half of the napkin back.

5b. The finished Diagonal Fold— incredibly simple, yet very lovely— can be placed on your plate .

3b.

4b.

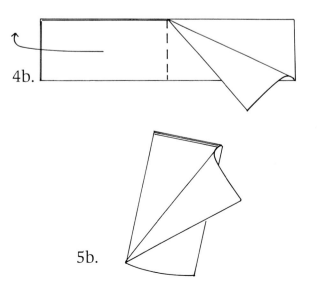

5b.

Bud

Uncomplicated and quick to make, yet elegant, the Bud is the ideal folded napkin form. This folding figure is extremely decorative, on either side, two large petals already seem to have opened, while on the inside, the bud perseveres in this very last moment before blossoming. Use napkins at least 16 by 16 inches in size so that this attractive form may fully come into bloom.

Folding Instructions

1. Spread out the napkin face down on the table. Thus the patterned or right side will be underneath. Fold in the middle, bringing the bottom edge up to the top edge to form a rectangle.

2. Bring the upper left and right corners diagonally down to meet at the center of the bottom edge.

3. The napkin lies now as a triangle in front of you. Fold the left and right corners diagonally up so that the corners meet on the upper tip.

4. Fold the corners of top flaps diagonally down and outward to meet the side corners.

5. The lower half of the napkin is now gracefully gathered so that it can be placed into a napkin ring.

3.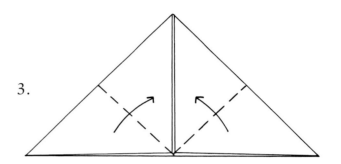

1.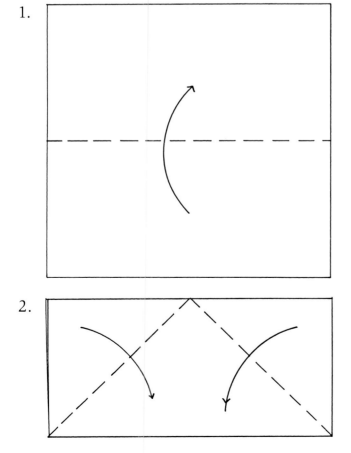

2.

4.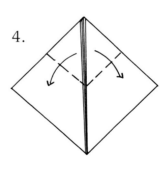

5.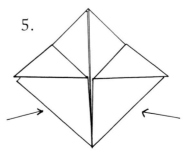

6. By gathering the lower half of the napkin in this way, the lateral petals and the bud in the center gently arch outward and up. The only thing left to do is to arrange the finished Bud on your plate.

6.

Little Swan

The Little Swan is a delightful figure, although it takes some time to execute and may require a bit of practice for perfection. Nevertheless, it is certainly worth the time and care involved. For whether made from colored paper napkins with airy feather dress for the coffee table or worked from fine fabric with elegant wing for festive meals, the Little Swan will be a success on any occasion.

In order for your Little Swan to turn out nicely, you should use a well-starched napkin so that the finished figure has sufficient stability. If you are using paper napkins, to keep the figure from spreading apart, insert the tines of a fork into the front end at the base of the neck. For best results remember to take the time to make sharp creases at each step of the folding so that the Little Swan has a slim and firm contour.

Folding Instructions

1. Begin with a napkin folded into quarters, turned to stand on its tip with the loose corners at the top. To fold a napkin into quarters, fold the napkin in half up into a rectangle, and then crossways in half, left over right, into a square. The loose four corners will be in the upper right. Paper napkins are usually prefolded in this manner. Now turn the napkin, folded into a square, so that it stands on its tip and has the loose corners at the top.

Now fold the bottom side edges diagonally in to meet at an imaginary vertical centerline.

2. The napkin should look like drawing 2. Turn the napkin over, keeping the sharp point at the bottom.

3. Now fold the bottom long side edges diagonally in to meet at an imaginary vertical centerline. The napkin should now look like drawing 4 before the next fold.

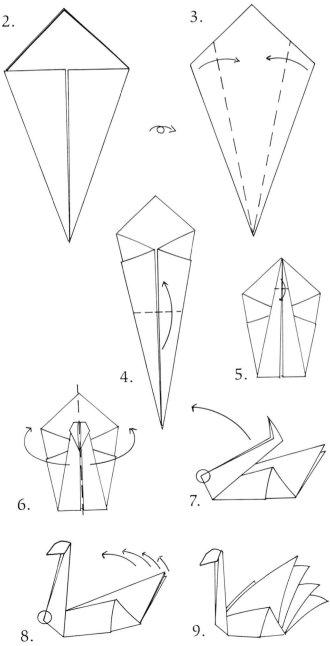

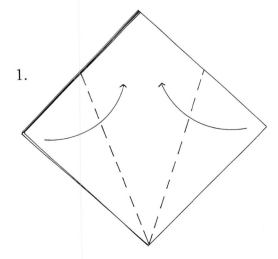

34

4. Fold the napkin horizontally in half, bringing the lower tip of the napkin up onto the upper tip.

5. The folded, narrow point on top is again folded down about ¾ to 1 inch below the top. This folded point will become the head of the Little Swan.

6. Fold the napkin in half along a vertical centerline so that the right and left sides bend back until they meet. Note that the head will remain on the outside. Remember to firmly smooth down the creases again and again.

7. Firmly hold the napkin together at its lower end and turn the figure sideways as shown in drawing 7. Hold the neck at the circle shown. With your other hand, carefully pull the neck of the Little Swan slightly outwards so that it forms right angle to the body.

Now press laterally in the area between head and neck in order to shape the head of the Little Swan.

8. Continue to hold the Little Swan at the base of the neck. With the other hand, reach below the individual layers at the tail end of the swan and carefully pull each one after the other, separately so that they ruffle like the plumage of a fluffy tail. To create space between the ruffles, it is helpful to slightly bend the lateral wings during this step.

9. You may now place the finished Little Swan onto a plate. As you place the figure, you should once more press the base of the neck onto the body and adjust the overall form of the Little Swan. In case your Little Swan needs additional support, you may carefully slide the base of the neck between the tines of a fork or tie a thin piece of ribbon around the neck.

Phoenix

In contrast to some of the more dramatic figures, it is the intricacy of this design that catches the eye. Here we have another of the traditional folds from the timeless art of napkin folding—the beautifully shaped Phoenix. Our Phoenix, however, does not rise from the ashes but rather must be folded by us; for this, we need a napkin at least 16 by 16 inches in size. By the way, you can get a very lovely effect for this form if the napkins you use have an edge with decorative trimming.

Folding Instructions

1. Spread out the napkin face down on the table in the shape of a diamond. Fold the four corners inward to meet at the center.

2. Turn the napkin over.

3. Now fold the napkin in half, bringing the top edge down to the bottom edge to form a rectangle.

4. Fold the left half of the napkin backwards so that it lies under the right half.

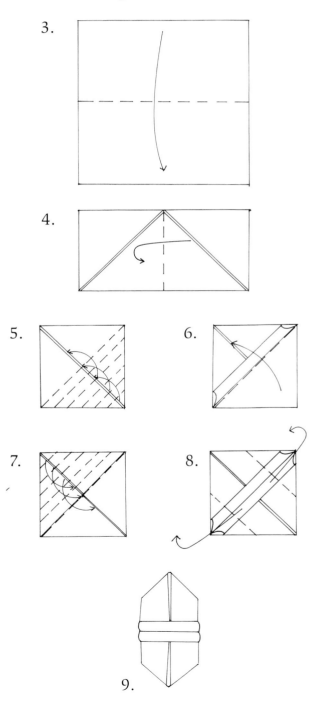

5. Now take the first layer of the lower right edge by the tip. Fold up this tip diagonally toward the upper left corner in a rolling fold, by which the corner is folded again and again to a width of about ½ to ¾ inch, until you reach the middle of the napkin. The creased part of the napkin forms a narrow band just above an imaginary line from the lower left corner to the upper right corner. Smooth the edges of the band down well.

6. Now fold the lower right corner of the next layer of the lower right half diagonally up to meet the upper left corner and smooth down the crease.

7. Take the upper left corner of the layer you just folded and fold up this tip diagonally toward the lower right corner, again and again a width of ½ to ¾ inch, until you reach just past the middle of the napkin revealing the first band. Now there are two parallel bands running from the lower left corner to the upper right corner. Smooth the edges of the new band down well.

8. Fold the lower left and upper right corners of the napkin behind to overlap at the back of the napkin.

9. Now arrange the finished Phoenix on your plate.

Winged Arrow

This napkin form is called the Winged Arrow. There are several variations on this theme, such as the Simple Arrow and the Arrowhead. This form, however, could also have been called the "Simple Arrow" as it is really easy and quick to make. The Winged Arrow is, in fact, the best example of a very interesting decoration that can be created in no time at all. The sharp pointed shape itself makes this figure exciting. Its beauty, however is expressed through the details of its inner shape—a lovely conical middle fold that sets a charming contrast to the zigzag of pointed corners. You will be able to produce an expressive Winged Arrow with cloth napkins 12 by 12 inches in size.

Paper napkins, do not work well unless you go through the trouble of slightly ironing them after the first folding step, otherwise one of the prefolded edges will run directly along the conical middle fold. It is precisely this middlle fold that should appear smooth and flawless.

Folding Instructions

1. Begin with an open napkin. Fold in the middle, bringing the top edge down to the bottom edge.

2. Now fold the upper left and right corners of the napkin diagonally down so that they meet at the center of the lower edge to form a triangle.

3. Take the corners that you just folded in, starting from the center of the lower edge, and fold them out diagonally to lie on top of the left and right edges of the triangle of the napkin.

4. Following this, push the entire napkin together starting from both edges, bringing the inner creases to meet at an imaginary centerline. By doing so, the smooth middle part bends up into a narrow fold.

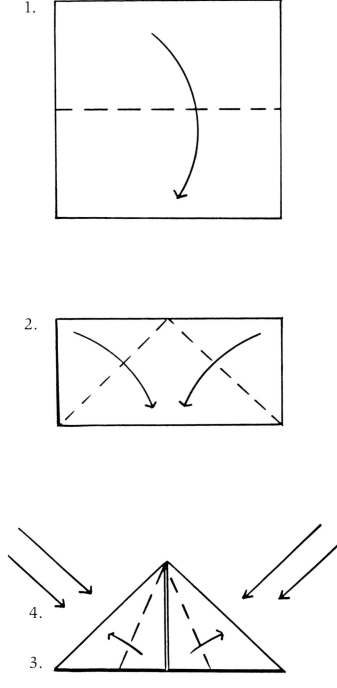

5. Firmly smooth down the standing middle fold, starting from the tip, so that it lies as a wide fold above the middle of the napkin.

6. Finally, the flat middle fold is given a rounded shape. The conical middle fold can be smoothed open by slightly pulling the napkin apart, carefully reaching into it from behind, and then rounding it up. Close the bottom of the napkin again and place the finished Winged Arrow on your plate.

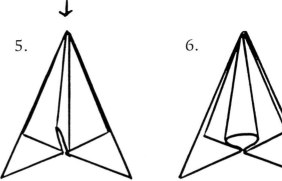

Shell

With a little imagination, the contours of this figure, with their opening, luxurious folds, can remind one of a shell. These lively folds give this napkin figure its particular charm. When set on stoneware dishes embellished with ocean motifs, as in our example, you'll have a table setting evocative of al fresco meals near the beach. Floral patterned or plain white dishes also work well with this beautiful shape. And you will find the Shell suitable for any occasion.

In folding this figure, keep in mind that our Shell will turn out too small unless the napkin is at least 16 by 16 inches in size. And use, if possible, cloth napkins. The firmly pre-embossed edges of the fold of paper and fleece napkins could disturb the appearance of the Shell, especially with single-colored napkin material. Furthermore, this figure, when folded from nice fabric, appears more voluptuous and its folds fall more generously and softly.

Folding Instructions

1. Begin with an open napkin. Fold in the middle, bringing the bottom edge up to the top edge.

2. Now fold the right and left sides sides in to meet at the center of the napkin.

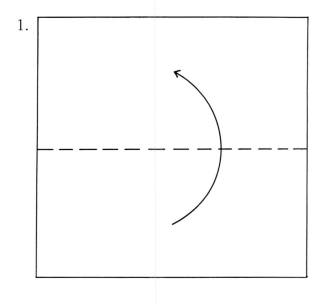

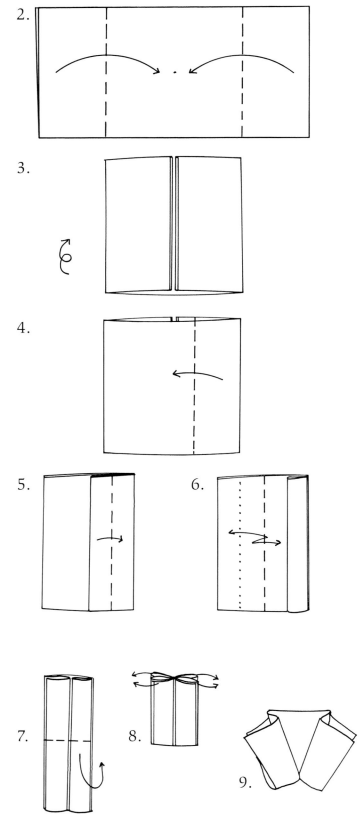

3. Turn the napkin over by flipping the bottom edge up to become the top edge. Make sure after turning it over that you now have the free edges of the napkin at the bottom.

4. Now fold in the right side about one-third of the width of the napkin.

5. Fold back in half the flap you just folded so that the left edge of that flap comes to lie precisely on top of the right edge of the napkin.

6. Fold the left part of the napkin, which is still smooth, in a similar fashion. The dashed line shows a forward crease and the dotted line a backward crease. That is, bring the left edge to the far right edge, and then fold back in half the flap you just folded so that its right edge comes to lie precisely on top of the new left edge of the napkin. The inner edges of the folded bands will meet at the center.

7. Next, fold the lower half of the napkin back so that the bottom edge comes to lie directly beneath the top edge. Smooth down the crease of this fold well.

8. In order for the Shell figure to fully develop, the free outer corners on the upper edge are now carefully pulled outwards. That is, both corners of the upper as well as the lower layers of cloth are pulled gently outward.

9. You can now place the Shell on your plate as the inner folds keep the figure slightly open in the desired shape.

Funny Fish

Next time you've extended an invitation for a fish dinner, if you want to have some fun, this napkin figure could add the perfect touch. You will be thrilled when you find out how quick and easy it is to prepare the Funny Fish "ready to serve." With the choice of an understated napkin material, this Funny Fish reveals itself as suitably modest—it is always a guaranteed success!

Folding Instructions

1. Spread out the napkin face down on the table in the shape of a diamond. Fold the napkin up in half, bringing the bottom corner to the top corner.

2. Fold up the bottom edge of the triangle forming a strip approximately 1¼ to 1½ inches wide.

3. Turn the napkin over, flipping the top point down to the bottom.

4. Fold the the left and the right sides of the napkin from the center of the upper edge diagonally down to meet at an imaginary centerline. The creased, narrow strips now rest as a double band lengthwise above the center of the napkin.

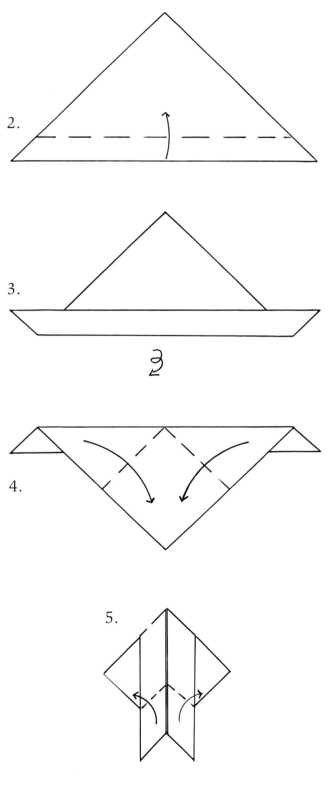

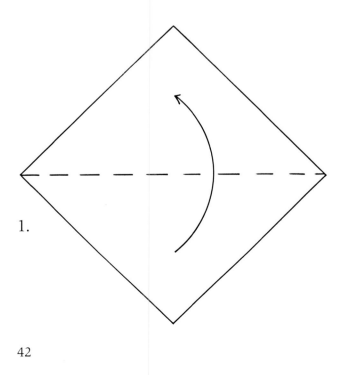

5. Now fold the two pointed tips of this band outwards as shown in drawings 5 and 6.

6. The Fish is already done at this point and only needs to be turned over.

7. Arrange the completed Funny Fish flat on your plate. A glass bead placed as an eye constitutes the final creative touch.

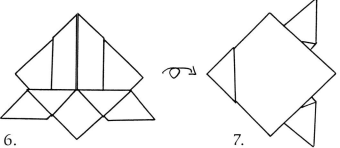

6.

7.

Peacock

The Peacock is a fine example of an elegant and impressive napkin figure that can be easily created without great artistic skills or complicated folding. Don't be afraid of this decorative napkin design — all you need are napkins 12 by 12 inches in size and some patience during folding. You will be delighted to find that this beautiful Peacock is most easily made from simple paper napkins. Whether you use plain solid-colored material in order to accentuate the decorative fold design of this figure, or napkins with a patterned design to suggest the shimmering beauty of the inspiration for the figure is entirely up to you.

Folding Instructions

1. Spread-out the napkin on the table in the shape of a diamond. The napkin should now be accordion-pleated from top to bottom; this will form diagonal creases of small zigzag folds. It is important that a mountain fold, that is, a fold whose crease points up, runs precisely through the left and right side corners of the napkin. As a beginner, it is best that you start by folding the entire napkin in half to get the center crease and then continue to alternately fold the two sides of the napkin, starting from the center crease with equal distances back and forth. We have drawn the mountain folds in drawing 1 as continuous lines and the valley folds (folds whose creases point down) as dashed lines.

2. Work very carefully. All folds should be of equal height. Therefore, always pay attention as you fold back and forth that the creases of the folds end precisely on top of one another.

3. After folding, the napkin should lie as a small band in front of you. In order for your napkin to get the nice sharp edges seen here, you should place this band flat in front of you and then firmly smooth down the creases of the folds once again.

   Then carefully fold up diagonally approximately one-third of the napkin on the left.

4. At exactly this diagonal crease, the Peacock figure is put deep within a narrow glass. In this way, the longer part of the napkin is slightly fanned open automatically and juts out above the rim of the glass like a wide train. The shorter, upper part of the napkin juts out of the glass to become the neck of the Peacock. To get the hint of a head, first bend the tip slightly down and then gently squeeze it at the sides together again.

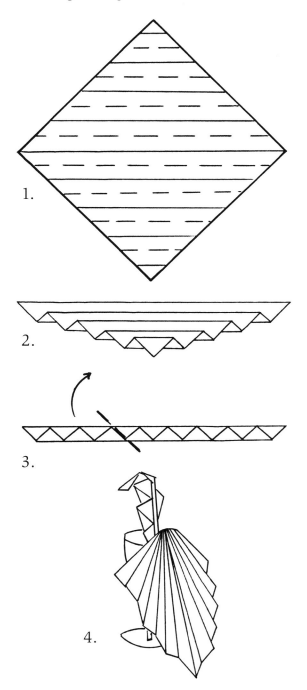

Origami Butterfly

The strict lines of this Butterfly and the folding technique hint that this figure may be derived from origami, the Japanese art of paper folding. Origami has so many beautiful, artistic forms to offer, yet it has only recently been looked to as a source for additions to the art of napkin folding. This attractive Origami Butterfly folded from light, colorful paper napkins, will be a guaranteed hit with your guests as a bright and cheerful messenger of spring.

Folding Instructions

1. Begin with an open napkin face-down on the table. Fold in the middle, bringing the bottom edge up to the top edge.

2. Fold the upper left and right corners diagonally down to meet at the center of the lower edge.

3. The napkin, which is now a triangle in front of you, is then turned over, flipping the left corner over to become the right.

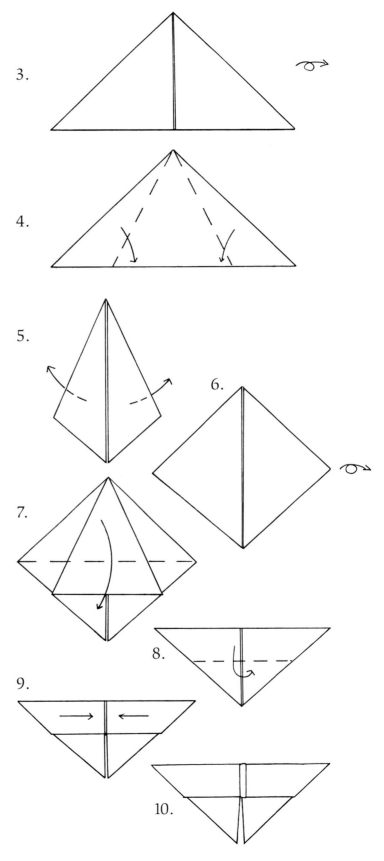

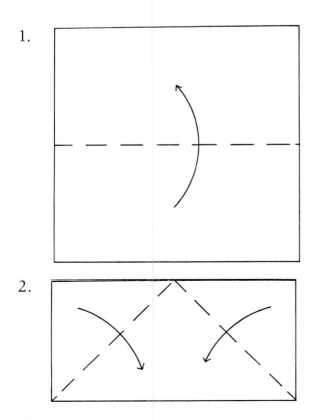

4. Fold in the left and right edges of the triangle diagonally to meet at an imaginary centerline.

5. The free corners that rest at the back center of the napkin are now pulled out sideways from under the napkin.

6. The napkin now lies in front of you as a square standing on its tip with two creases running beside each other along an imaginary centerline. At this point, the figure is once again turned over, flipping the left corner over to become the right corner.

7. Fold the napkin in half, bringing the top corner down to the bottom corner, to form a triangle.

8. Fold the lower tip of the very top layer inside, tucking it under the top flap. This reveals the two free tips below.

9. Finally, shape the body of the Origami Butterfly by squeezing the napkin figure together from the sides toward the center. In doing so, the material at the inner the edges of the wings near the centerline should arch slightly up. The bottom tips will also spread slightly apart.

10. The finished Origami Butterfly rests in front of you, ready to be placed on your plate.

Violet

The beauty and variety of flowers have been an inspiration to every generation of napkin-folding artists. The many attractive figures in the form of stylized flowers are among their most astonishing creations. Here I present the decorative Violet with its soft, flowing contours and airy petals.

In order for your Violet to succeed in all its glory, you should use napkins at least 16 by 16 inches in size. The best results come with the use of paper or thin fabric that will express the tenderness of this figure. This Violet napkin form needs some support by means of a napkin ring, a narrow glass, or the tines of a fork to achieve suitable stability.

Folding Instructions

1. Spread the napkin face-down in front of you so it stands on its tip in a diamond shape. Thus, if you are using printed material, the patterned side is underneath. Fold the napkin in half horizontally, bringing the top corner down to the bottom corner.

2. The napkin now lies as a triangle in front of you with the point at the bottom. Fold the left and right corners diagonally down to meet on the lower tip. The two halves of the former upper edge now meet precisely at an imaginary centerline.

3. The new form once again corresponds to a square standing on its tip in a diamond shape. Next, fold this square in half horizontally, by bringing the lower tip of the figure to the upper tip.

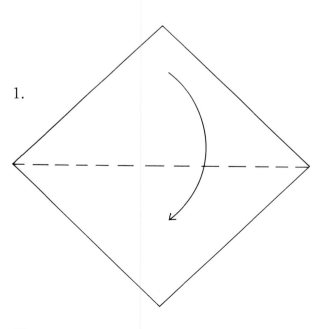

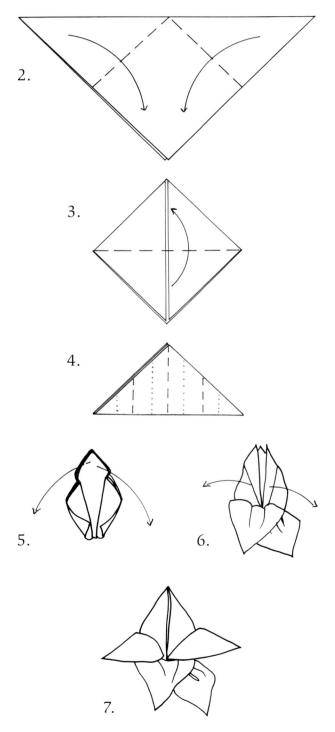

48

4. Fold the triangle thus created along the lower edge from left to right in about three to five equal folds by folding the napkin alternately back and forth in an accordion pleat.

5. Hold the gathered end firmly in your hand and pull the tip at the very front; in other words, the tip of the triangle of the very top layer is carefully folded forward and down to the right. The tip of the next layer is similarly pulled down; however, this is adjusted slightly more to the left.

6. After this, spread the free tips of the narrow wings, which have become visible by now, bending them forward and pulling them to the outside.

7. At last, the airy petals are given their final shape and are brought into position, and the finished Violet is put into a napkin ring or gently tucked into a narrow glass. Another possibility is similar to the support given to the Little Swan; the figure is slid between the tines at the very end of a fork.

Little Horn

Perhaps when you first see this napkin's shape, you might recognize it as the the classic cone form. In this charming version, the simple cone with offset pointed edges, here called the Little Horn, might be less familiar to you. When the cone is fanned open, with offset tips, the figure becomes less static, gains lightness, and softens in its appearance in a very appealing way. This multilayered and interesting run of offset edges can be emphasized with lace or patterned borders; however, plain solid-colored napkins, whether cloth or paper, receive not only a certain presence of shape, but also an attractive outer appearance when folded into the Little Horn. If you use paper napkins for your Little Horn, these must be completely colored on both sides, since with this folding technique both the front and back of the material become visible.

Folding Instructions

1. Begin with an open napkin. Fold in the middle, bringing the top edge down to the bottom edge to form a rectangle.

2. Now, fold the napkin once crossways again into a square. Paper napkins are already folded in this manner. In this case, the four loose corners are at the lower right.

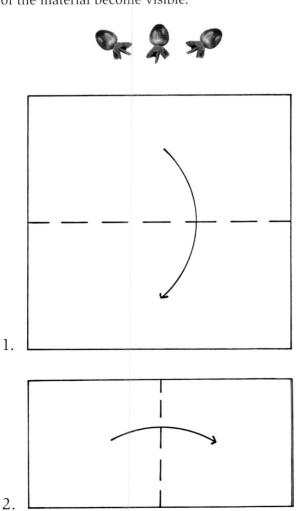

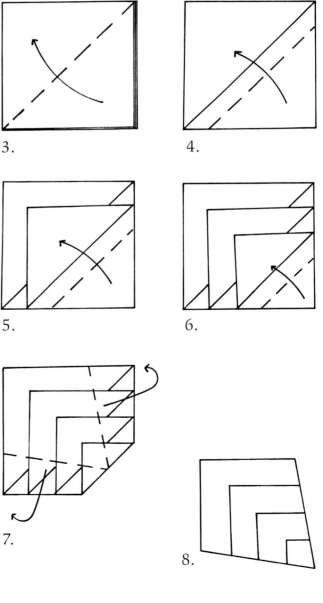

3. The napkin now lies as a square in front of you, and the lower right corner reveals four free tips that rest on top of one another. Grab the tip of the very top layer and fold it diagonally up onto the upper left corner of the napkin.

4. Grab the second tip at the lower right and again fold it diagonally toward the upper left; however, it should be ¾ to 1¼ inch below the first tip.

5. Take the next tip and fold it also diagonally to the upper left in such a way that the tip comes to rest offset an equal distance to the second one as the second was to the first.

6. Fold the last tip from the lower right in a similar manner so the tip is offset the same distance as the previous ones.

7. Now fold the bottom and right sides of the napkin back so that they create the shape of a pointed cone, along the center of which run equally offset tips.

8. The finished Little Horn can be draped over your plate.

Necktie

Nowadays, dinners have become less formal and allow for a touch of whimsy. Thus, some new forms of napkin figures have popped up and been added to our repertoire. These have taken napkin folding in fresh and fanciful directions of form and color. Decorations do not always have to be simply formal or elegant, but can go beyond festive to sardonic and silly. As an amusing example of these new dinner companions, here I would like to introduce to you the uncomplicated Necktie. Colorful patterns or funny motifs in the napkin itself, as depicted in our example, underline the whimsical character of the Necktie.

Folding Instructions

1. Spread a napkin in front of you in a diamond shape, turned on its tip. The patterned side should lie face down. Fold the sides, starting from the upper tip, each about one-third inward toward the center. The left and right edges of the napkin and the creases of these folds should align exactly with one another. Smooth the edges down well.

2. The sides of the napkin are now once again folded in the same manner, starting from the upper tip, about one-third of the width in on top of each other. Pay attention that the lower tip and the upper tip lie precisely along an imaginary vertical center-line. Smooth the edges down well.

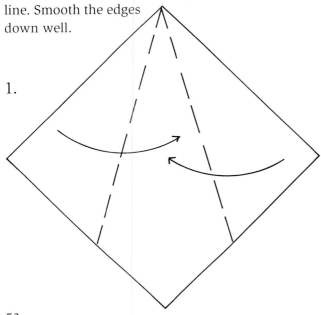

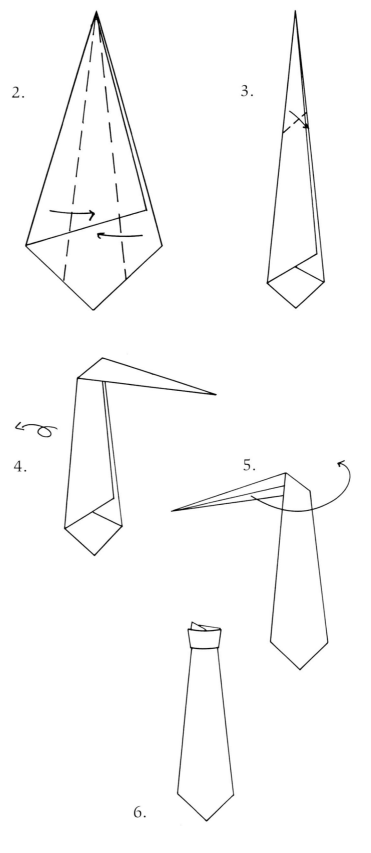

3. Fold the upper tip about one-third of its length, diagonally toward the right.

4. Now turn the napkin figure over, bringing the right point to become the left.

5. The narrow tip that juts out to the left from under the napkin is now loosely wound around the upper

end of the napkin, just like the knot for a tie. The end is then tucked on the back side from below into the fold.

6. Finally, drape the finished Tie over your plate.

Bow Tie

As companion to the straight Necktie, the Bow Tie with its rather playful effect is presented here. As opposed to the modern Necktie, the Bow Tie figure comes from a long tradition. Yet, it not only makes an elegant statement when made from fine cloth held by a napkin ring and placed on expensive china, but also when made from bright paper as a festive table decoration.

Folding Instructions

1. Spread out a napkin on the table in front of you with the patterned side face down. Now fold all four corners diagonally inward to meet at the center.

2. Repeat this procedure once again—folding each outside corner in to meet at the center.

3. Now fold two opposite corners of the napkin toward the center. The folded corners should touch once again above the center of the napkin.

4. Turn the napkin over. Gather the folded napkin together and slide a napkin ring over one of the pointed ends of the napkin to the middle.

5. All that's left to do is to finesse the Bow Tie into its final shape. To do this, reach from behind under the napkin and slightly pull out the gathered sides with their pointed corners. Now place the finished Bow Tie on your plate.

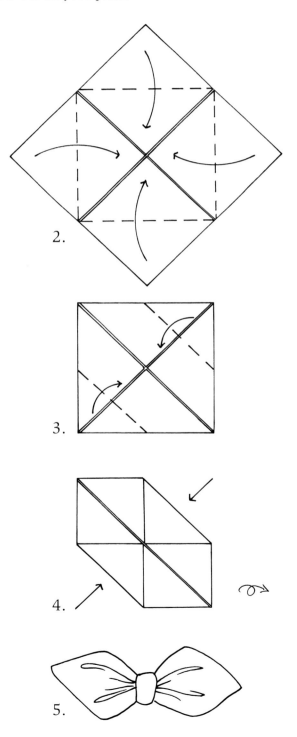

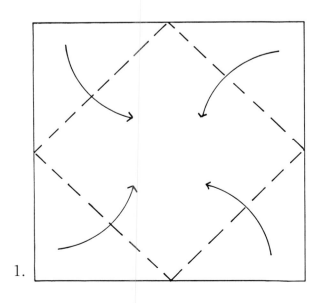

Shirt

Now that you have already gotten to know the Necktie and the Bow Tie, I do not wish to keep the original Shirt from you. This is an unconventional design that's sure to brighten a child's birthday party, especially when made from colorful paper napkins with funny patterns. Slightly more discreet, the shirt becomes a whimsical eye catcher at a meal with good friends. If you use fine linen, you can spruce up the Shirt by adding small satin bows. Your napkins will become whimsical decorations appropriate for formal dinners. An unusual table decoration might alternate the Necktie, Bow Tie, and Shirt, or, more simply, the Necktie and Shirt.

Folding Instructions

1. If you are using large cloth napkins, begin by folding each outside corner diagonally in to meet at the center. This helps reduce the size of the napkin. Should you use paper napkins 12 by 12 inches in size, begin with step 3.

2. Turn the napkin so that it again looks like a square.

3. Fold the left and right sides of the napkin one-fourth in so that the edges meet above an imaginary centerline.

4. At the upper edge fold an approximately ¾-inch wide strip backward.

5. Then fold the upper edges narrowly, more or less as shown in drawing 5, diagonally forward. In this way, you create the collar. Smooth down the edges of the fold well so that the collar stays in place.

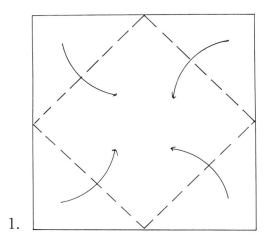

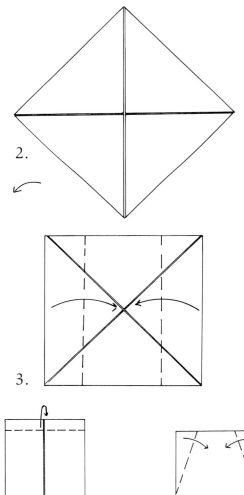

6. The lower free corners of the top layer are now folded, starting from the center of the lower edge, diagonally outward.

In this way, you begin to create the short sleeves of the Shirt.

7. The lower half of the napkin is now simply folded up and the edge slid under the corners of the collar.

8. Depending on the occasion, you can finish off the Shirt with a small bow tie made from ribbon.

6.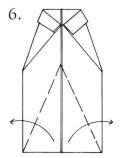

7.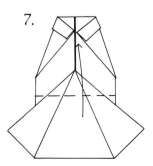

8.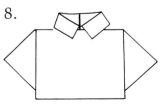

Cornucopia

As the name suggests, this Cornucopia is well suited to being filled. It's ideal for parites; you can slide place cards, flowers, or little presents inside the folds. As it can be made very quickly and easily from paper napkins, you should certainly try out this decorative idea. Pretty trimmings, fine hem-stitches, or playful edges of lace have a particularly great effect with this simple but impressive-looking figure.

Folding Instructions

1. Begin with the napkin spread out face down on the table in front of you so that it stands on its tip, in the shape of a diamond. Then bring the bottom corner over the top, folding the napkin up in half into a triangle. Smooth down the crease well.

2. Fold the left and right corners up diagonally so that they meet at the top corner and the edges lie along an imaginary centerline. Again remember to smooth down the creases well.

3. Fold the left and right corners of the napkin in diagonally, starting from the lower tip, towards the center so that the former edges meet vertically above the imaginary centerline of the napkin. Once again, smooth down the creases well.

4. The napkin rests now as a narrow kite-like shape in front of you. At this point all you need to do is take the two ends of upper layer of the napkin, which rest on the tip, and fold them down over the edge of the sides just folded in.

5. Arrange the finished Cornucopia on a plate and, according to your taste, slide silverware, a flower, a name card, or other decoartions into the pocket.

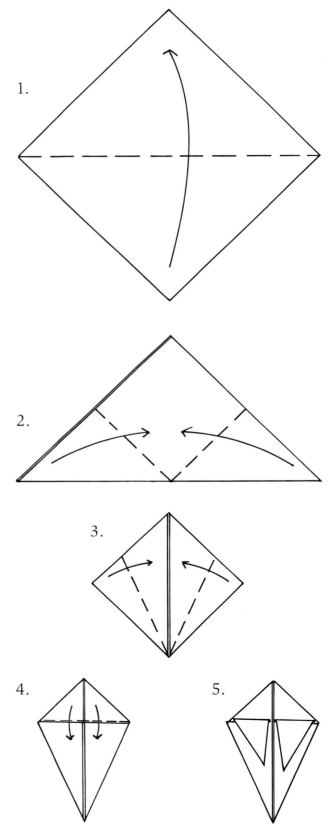

1.

2.

3.

4.

5.

Diamond in the Square

The Diamond in the Square, although it is a rather simple napkin form, nevertheless radiates a certain elegance through its noble understatement. A clever folding technique makes the napkin appear to be two staggered squares that lie on top of one another. This compact napkin form with its bold geometric effect is the ideal decorative element for all minimalist, modern table arrangements. While you can use napkins as small as 12 by 12 inches for the Diamond, a napkin size of 16 by 16 inches and larger is more effective. Paper or cloth napkins with embossed edges or borders should be avoided, if possible, for this figure; they would disrupt the appearance of the napkin. This interesting design is shown to its best advantage when made from plain cloth napkins in a color that contrasts with the color of your dinnerware.

Folding Instructions

1. Spread out a napkin in front of you as a square. Fold it in thirds, the lower third up and the upper third down, as you would fold a letter. Smooth down the edges of the fold well and then turn the napkin over.

2. Starting from the center of the top edge, fold the left side of the napkin diagonally down so that the former upper edge comes to rest precisely vertically above the former centerline of the napkin.

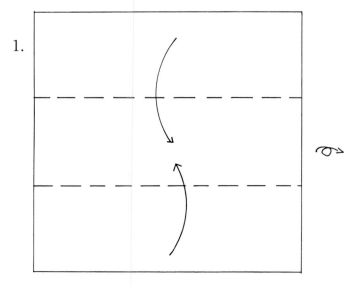

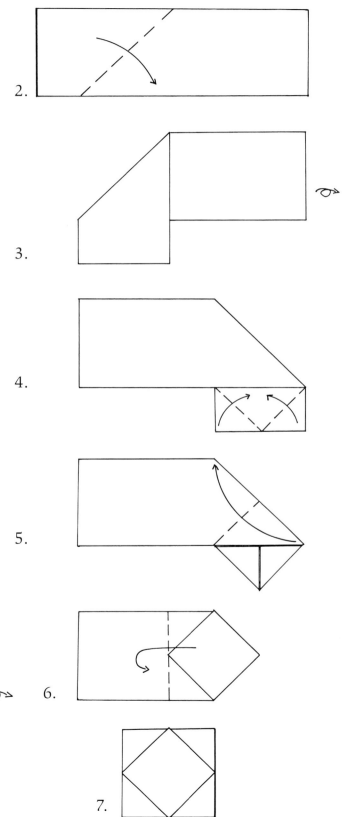

3. Turn the napkin over once more so that the slanted edge is on the right.

4. Fold both corners of the end that juts out from under the napkin diagonally up to the folded edge of the napkin.

5. The tip thus created can be seen as the corner of a small square—or diamond. This square shape is folded up to the left diagonally in such a way that the outer right corner of the napkin is folded onto the upper right corner of the napkin.

6. A small diamond shape has just been created that rests on the napkin; however, this is still on the right side of the napkin.

To place the diamond in the center of the napkin, the left half of the napkin is now simply folded backward so that the crease lies exactly in a vertical line along the outer left corner of the diamond.

7. The Diamond in the Square now rests precisely above the center of the napkin with the straight edge of the napkin that was just folded back lying exactly at the outer right corner of the diamond.

Bent Leaf

The gracefully Bent Leaf is one of the newer figures in the art of napkin folding. The strictly stylized, yet graceful, light form makes one think that there may be influences of origami, the ancient Japanese art of paper folding, behind it. Though this may be the case, the Bent Leaf nonetheless reveals itself as a modern napkin form, which, in the spirit of the times, can be quicky and effortlessly folded from any kind of napkin material, adapts with its simple elegance to any occasion and any table decoration, and creates a stunning display on any kind of china. Thus, the Bent Leaf is a versatile napkin figure that impresses the beholder with its simple beauty.

Folding Instructions

1. Spread out the napkin on the table in the shape of a diamond. The patterned side should face down. Fold the napkin in half, bringing the left corner over the right corner so that the long side is at the left.

2. First, gently bring the lower point up toward the upper point, with the fold running horizontally through the right corner. However, do not smooth down the folded edge, but rather shift the folded point in such a way that it comes to rest slightly shifted towards the right of what will become the left upper point. Only after this shift is the folded edge, which has slightly moved up on the left, smoothed down well.

3. Now fold the lower right corner up diagonally, in such a way that its point is also shifted to the right of what will become the center point by an equal distance as the center is from the far left point.

4. Fold the right corner of the folded napkin figure backward, in such a way that the crease will run from the lower tip to the center of the right side of the third point that was just folded up.

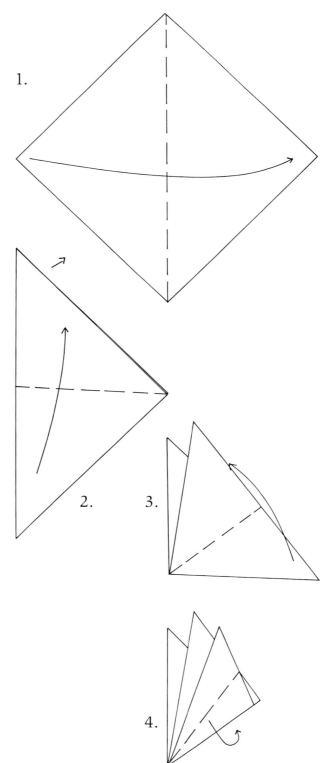

5. The folded napkin should appear as a narrow fan in front of you and only has to be draped in its expressive pose as the Bent Leaf. To do this, the lower part of the napkin is simply folded diagonally backward.

6. Finally, bring the Bent Leaf into the right position with a quarter turn clockwise.

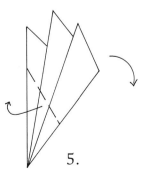

5.

6.

Candle

The Candle, appropriately done in dark burgundy, is presented in a festive manner, as its form is the perfect ornament for a holiday season table. But this napkin may certainly be used for other occasions as well. Folded in white fabric, the Candle is an elegant table decoration for any dinner party; done in a cheerful color or even several colors, it's just right for a birthday table. The Candle receives its style through a small corner of fabric that is brought into shape at the very end to suggest a flickering flame. A cloth napkin that is well ironed, perhaps with a little starch, gives the Candle its necessary support.

Folding Instructions

1. Spread out the napkin face down on the table in the shape of a diamond. Fold the napkin up in half, bringing the bottom corner to the top corner.

2. Fold up the bottom edge of the triangle, forming a strip approximately ⅝ to ¾ inch wide.

3. Turn the napkin over, flipping the left corner over to the right.

4. Then fold the upper point horizontally down to the center of the bottom edge.

5. Now fold back the flap that was just folded down, bringing it horizontally up in such a way that the point juts out about ¾ to 1 inch above the upper edge of the napkin.

6. Fold the left side of the napkin toward the right. The crease should run vertically exactly from that spot where the upper flap juts out over the edge, as in drawing 6.

7. The entire napkin is now firmly rolled up from left to right until there is only a tiny tip sticking out at the lower end.

8. Diagonally fold up this small remaining tip and tuck it from above into the thicker edge of the napkin.

9. The tip of cloth that juts out on the upper end, that suggests the flame of the Candle, only needs to be gently shaped for it to "flicker" really nicely.

1.

2.

3.

4.

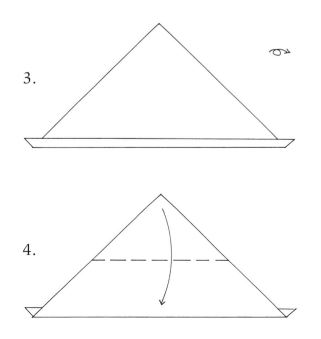

5.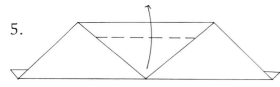

6.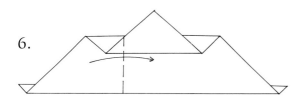

7.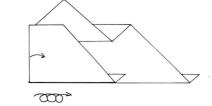

8.

9.

Christmas Tree

The holiday season is certainly a time for decorating as the entire family gathers around the festive table. This time of year calls the use of festive napkin forms, not only on very special days such as for Christmas dinner, but also on other days to add a holiday touch to the entire season. The Christmas Tree figure appears in several variations; however, the iconic tree form, which you will get to know here, is one of the more elegant realizations. Whether you use paper napkins in colorful, festive patterns or stay true to style with fine green cloth, decorated with small accessories as I have here, is entirely up to you.

Folding Instructions

1. Spread out a napkin in front of you as a square. If you are using printed napkins, the patterned side should face down. Now fold the napkin down in half horizontally, bringing the top edge down to the bottom edge to form a rectangle.

2. Fold once crossways again into a square, by creasing the napkin vertically along an imaginary centerline, and bringing the left edge to the right. Paper napkins are already folded in this manner. In this case, the four loose corners are at the lower right. Now rotate the napkin in front of you, so that the four loose corners point down.

3. The square should lie in front of you as a diamond on its tip with the loose corners pointing down. Now fold the sides of the napkin in to meet at the center.

4. Turn the napkin over, keeping the narrow point at the top.

5. Now fold the upper outer edges once more in to meet at the center. Then gently reach under the napkin, coming from the side, and pull the folded sides from under the napkin outward.

6. Now you only need to fold the lower triangular tip backward so the trunk of the Christmas Tree has a flat bottom edge.

7. Arrange the finished Christmas Tree on your plate and, if you like, decorate it with festive accessories, such as glitter and little stars.

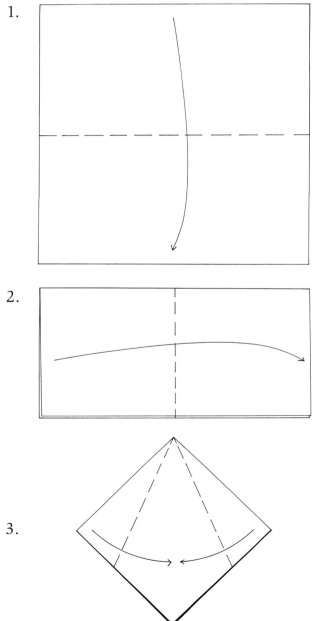

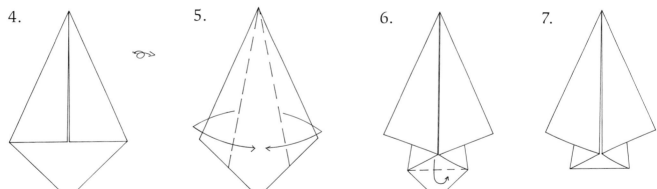

4. 5. 6. 7.

Pointed Roof

Folded from cotton napkins in a brightly colored check design, the Pointed Roof would be at home on the breakfast table or at a casual supper. Folded from fine damask, this figure also works well on a formal dinner table.

Whatever your choice of napkin, the Pointed Roof, with its refined elegance, belongs to those napkin figures that embody haute table culture in its purest form. After all, it is no accident that this figure is among the favorites of many restaurateurs and hoteliers.

The Pointed Roof has a particularly stylish effect when folded from a large cloth napkin; however, even paper napkins that are 12 by 12 inches in size work well with this stylish shape. A napkin with a colored border that contrasts with the dominant color is especially effective with this design. The border highlights the characteristics of this figure, creating a distinctive look.

Folding Instructions

1. Begin with the napkin spread out face down on the table in front of you so that it stands on its tip, in the shape of a diamond. Then bring the bottom corner over the top, folding the napkin up in half into a triangle.

2. Fold the left and right corners up diagonally so that they meet at the top corner and the edges lie along an imaginary centerline.

3. Turn the napkin over, flipping the top corner down to become the bottom corner.

4. Fold the top folded layer of the upper third of the napkin toward the bottom, as in drawing 4.

5. Fold the right and left sides backward until they meet.

6. Allow the napkin to open slightly and the Pointed Roof is created. The only thing left is to arrange it on your plate.

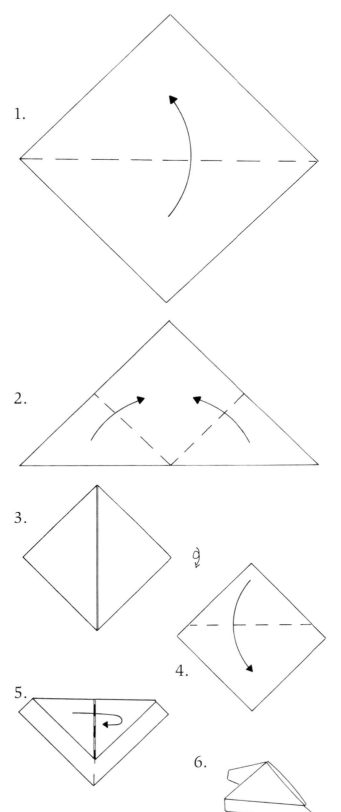

Jabot

A jabot is a softly falling lace or cloth frill attached to a neckband, which once decorated the front of a man's shirt as the fashionable rage in the 18th century. Much later the jabot appeared once more as romantic trimmings of pleated frill down the center front of a woman's blouse or dress. However, these playful accessories have also served as inspiration to the art of napkin folding. A narrow, rather straight silhouette, with a wide, divided tip stands in charming contrast to the Jabot's overall soft appearance.

A Jabot can be folded from paper napkins 12 by 12 inches in size. The imitated frills are shown to better advantage, and more true to style, when the Jabot is folded from soft cloth napkins that are 16 by 16 inches or larger.

Folding Instructions

1. Spread out the napkin face down so that it stands on its tip, in the shape of a diamond. Then bring the bottom corner over the top, folding the napkin up in half into a triangle.

2. Fold the sides of the triangle, starting from the upper tip, diagonally inward so that the side edges meet vertically above an imaginary centerline.

3. Fold the upper sides once again from the upper tip inward to meet at the centerline.

4. Fold the upper tip back by folding the napkin in about half backward. Then turn the napkin over.

5. Bend the long center tip back, tucking it behind the edge that runs across the napkin to secure it from unfolding. Then turn the napkin back over.

6. The finished Jabot is ready for you to arrange on your plate.

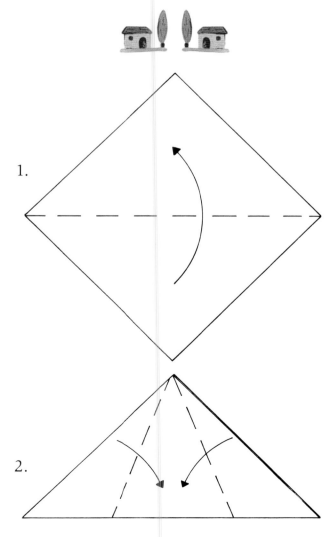

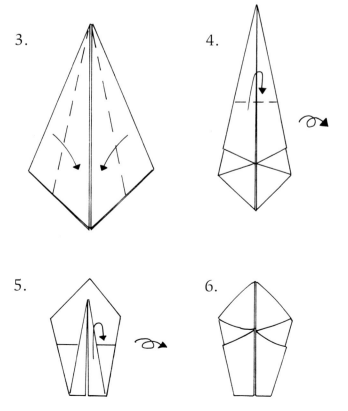

Double Diamond

At first glance, you might think this figure is not a very exciting napkin form. However, when you have a closer look at it, the subtle refinement of this napkin figure is revealed; two smaller diamonds lie atop and, at the same time, encompass the overall diamond shape.

The Double Diamond has a sophisticated look that is at home on a table with classic formality or modern verve. If you are now wondering how this bold geometric effect is achieved, let me reassure you that the folding technique is quite simple. Go ahead and try it yourself. You will achieve the best results with a solid-color cloth napkin about 16 by 16 inches in size.

Folding Instructions

1. With the right side face down, spread out the napkin in front of you. Fold the napkin vertically in half, bringing the right edge to left edge to form a rectangle.

2. Fold the upper corners diagonally in to meet at the center, and fold the lower corners, in the same way, diagonally in to meet at the center. Smooth the creases down well.

3. Bring the upper tip down and the lower tip up to meet at the center.

4. Turn the napkin over.

5. Now fold all four corners diagonally inward to meet at the center of the napkin.

6. After you have smoothed down the creases very well, you only need to turn the napkin over once more.

7. The Double Diamond is now complete.

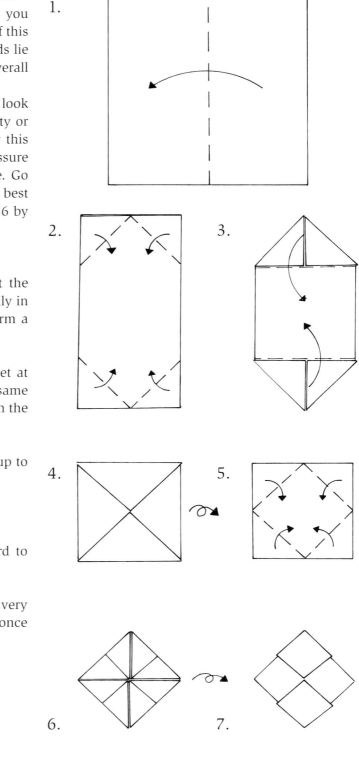

Lady's Slipper

Decorative flowers have always been a favorite motif for the art of napkin folding. Exotic flowers, such as lilies and orchids, have particularly inspired the imagination of napkin artists for they exist in innumerable variations. Thus, the Lady's Slipper, a native species of orchid, has also found its parallel in the art of napkin folding.

The Lady's Slipper figure is a fluid interpretation of the flower with its typical slipper-like petals. Each napkin so artistically shaped becomes an expressive ornament that gives a very special touch to your table, whether made from paper napkins for the kitchen table or made of fine fabric for a festive dinner. Try it yourself! You will be surprised how effectively the Lady's Slipper can be used. And you will be enthusiastic once you find how simply and easily this beautiful figure can be created!

Folding Instructions

1. Spread out the napkin face down so that it stands on its tip, in the shape of a diamond. Then bring the bottom corner over the top, folding the napkin up in half into a triangle.

2. Fold the left and right corners diagonally up so that they are at the same height as, but slightly to the sides of, the top point. The left and right points should be about 2½ inches apart.

3. Now fold the lower part of the napkin about one-third of the way up.

4. Afterward, accordion-pleat the napkin into 5 wide, well-proportioned folds. To make sure that a mountain fold, that is a fold whose crease points forward towards you, runs exactly vertically through the center tip, fold the napkin in the middle and then fold sides back and forth.

5. Hold the fanned napkin firmly together at the lower edge. In order to unfold the entire beauty of the Lady's Slipper, carefully pull the small tip in the front forward and down and then the two long side tips outward.

6. Tuck the base of the flower in a napkin ring or narrow glass for support. Gently give the petals of the Lady's Slipper their final shape.

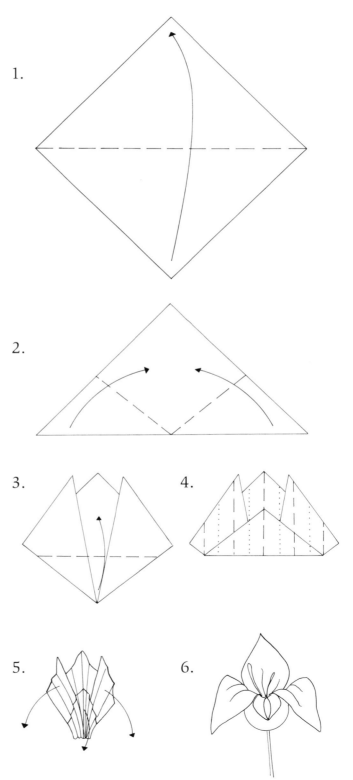

74

Angel

This attractive Angel will get your guests into the right mood for all the heavenly culinary delights that await them!

Create the Angel figure using firmer cotton cloth napkins—you may find that experimenting with color suits this figure well.

Folding Instructions

1. Spread the napkin with the right side down so that it stands on its tip, in the shape of a diamond. Then bring the top corner over the bottom, folding the napkin down in half into a triangle.

2. Fold the sides of the triangle, starting from the middle of the top edge, diagonally inward so that the former top edges meet at the center above an imaginary centerline.

3. Fold the upper left and right edges, from the upper tip, diagonally inward to meet at the center-line.

4. Fold the lower half of the napkin back, bringing the bottom tip behind to the upper tip.

5. Then fold the napkin vertically in half from right to left and smooth down the crease very well.

6. Place the figure on its lower edge, which you now allow to open to an obtuse angle. The completed Angel unfolds its wings all by itself.

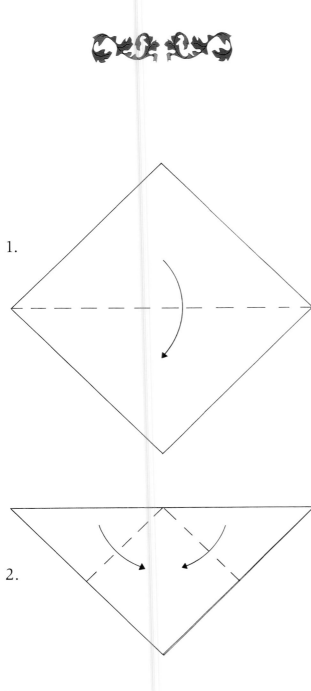

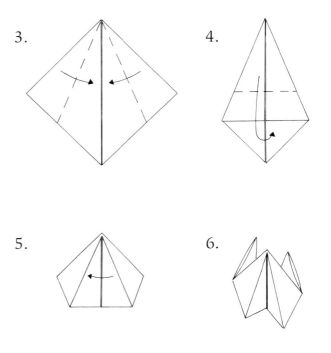

Sweetheart

For all invitations that come from the heart, it goes without saying that you would arrange the table decorations with loving care. The Sweetheart not only provides the perfect touch, but it is also quick and easy to fold. Even ordinary paper napkins can be transformed into this cute shape with just a few simple tricks. Romantic or playful patterns, such as the rose design in our example, are just right for this charming folding idea.

For the folding of this little heart, you should only use napkins up to a size of about 12 by 12 inches so that the result is not too big and flat.

Folding Instructions

1. Place the napkin spread out in front of you. The right or patterned side should face down. Fold the napkin horizontally up in half, bringing the bottom edge over the top edge.

2. Loosely drape the right side of the napkin up to the left, by gently folding diagonally up along a line from the center point of the lower edge to a point on the upper edge, which is in about one-fourth the width of the napkin. That is to say, fold as if along the broken line in drawing 2.

3. The left side of the napkin is now loosely folded toward the right over the diagonal edge of the folded part of the napkin. The bottom edge should come up to exactly coincide with the right diagonal edge of the folded napkin. As the napkin has only been loosely folded up to this point, you may in this step still make slight adjustments until you have a beautiful, well-proportioned heart lying in front of you.

4. If you are satisfied with the result, you may then slightly smooth down the side edges in order to help the Sweetheart keep its shape and then nicely arrange it on a plate.

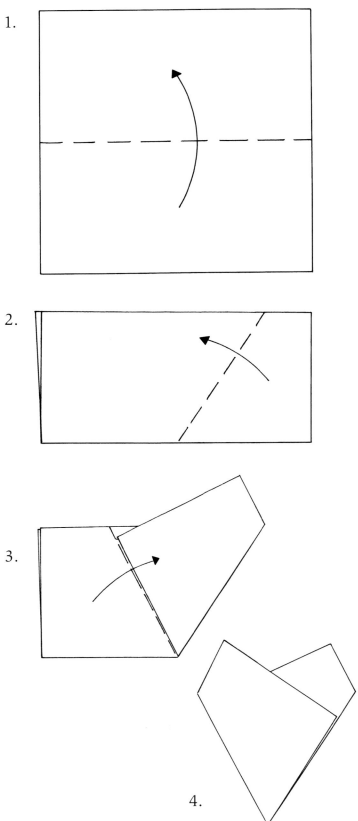

Chapeau

A Chapeau, as most everyone knows and can see when looking at this beautiful napkin figure, is purely and simply a hat. It is not half bad, this little French hat with the saucy brim whether made from fine cloth napkins for a good first impression or of beautifully patterned paper for everyday use. I take my hat off to this curiously handsome fellow.

Folding Instructions

1. Spread the napkin out as a square with the right or patterned side face down. Now fold the napkin horizontally in its half, bringing the bottom edge up to the top edge to form a rectangle.

2. Afterwards, fold the upper left corner diagonally down to the middle of the lower edge and the lower right corner up in a mirror-like fashion to lie at the former middle of the upper edge.

3. The napkin should now look like drawing 3. To get to the next folding step, the napkin must be turned in a particular way onto its reverse side by flipping it over to the right. What is important, so the napkin is correctly placed in front of you for the next step, is to notice that the top right corner becomes the lower left corner, and the right side is now the bottom edge.

4. With the napkin now positioned lengthwise in front of you, simply bring the top edge to the bottom edge by folding down horizontally in half.

5. As you folded the top edge down in half, there is an upper left point below that is now revealed. The corresponding right folded tip should gently be opened out from under the edge of the fold, if it has not already naturally done so. The left side of the napkin is now folded inward along a vertical line through the left upper tip, and the former left corner is tucked below the right triangular tip.

6. Now fold the right side of the napkin backward in the same manner, along a vertical line through the right upper tip. Here, the former right tip is also tucked between the folded half of the left tip behind and the middle.

8. The upper tips are then carefully turned inside out. For this, hold the napkin at its lower edge so that the tucked-in ends remain in place. Turn the napkin upside down.

9. To give the Chapeau its final shape, simply reach in between the two layers of fabric that make up the upper edge and carefully spread them apart. With a little care, place the Chapeau on your plate.

1.
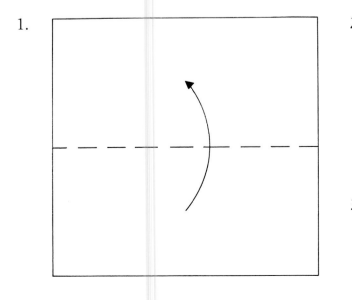

2.

3.
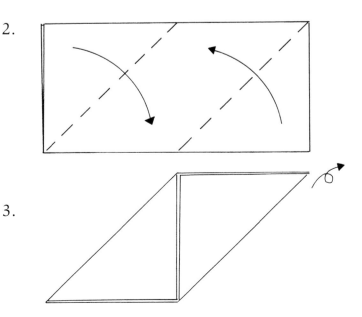

4.

5.

6.

7.

8.

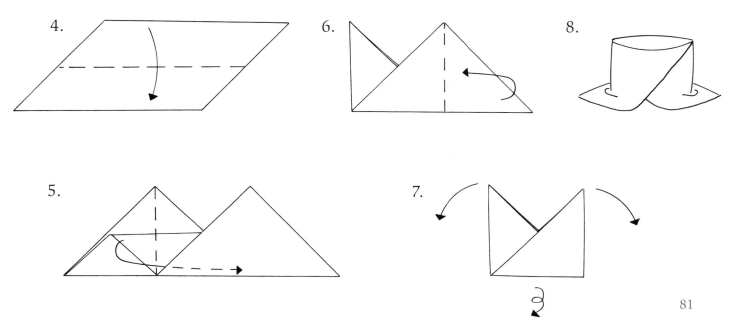

Tulip

Entirely different than many of the beautiful, three-dimensional and often also time-consuming designs depicted in this book, yet at the same time no less charming, this simply stylized Tulip is a stunning example of a flat napkin form.

This attractive and simple design not only catches the eye with understated elegance, but also proves to be extremely adaptable. Created from fine cloth napkins 16 by 16 inches in size, the Tulip turns into a striking statement that brings a touch of class to any great table. Folded from colorful paper napkins, the Tulip is a delightful springtime accent to your less formal gatherings.

Folding Instructions

1. Spread the napkin with the right or patterned side down so that it stands on its tip, in the shape of a diamond. Then bring the top corner down over the bottom, folding in half to form a triangle.

2. Fold the the lower tip of the triangle up to the middle of the upper edge.

3. Fold the pointed sides diagonally down so that they overlap, as shown in drawings 3 and 4.

4. The two tips that overlap at the lower end of the napkin are now each folded up along a line that matches the lower edge that lies beneath.

5. Fold the sides backward along a diagonal line and tuck them behind into one another.

6. Now you can lay the finished Tulip flat across your plate.

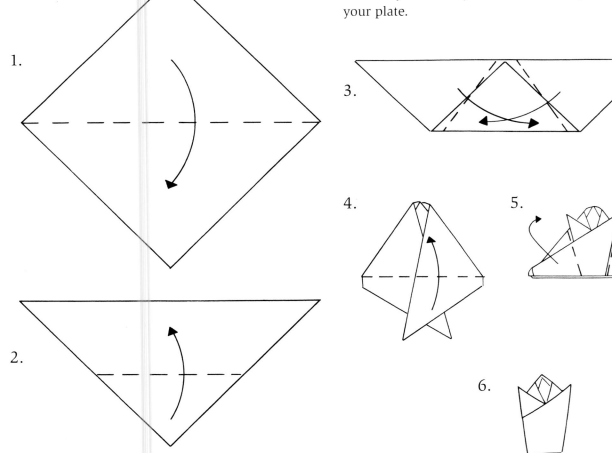

Jumping Frog

With a little imagination, this figure is indeed a Jumping Frog with a diamond-shaped body and firm hind legs. If you don't see it this way, it's still an intriguing napkin form with a lot of charm.

So, let it be whatever you like! Try your luck with this unusual napkin creation. Choose a cloth napkin at least 16 by 16 inches in size, for although the Jumping Frog is not difficult, the folding process reduces the size.

Folding Instructions

1. Spread the napkin with the right or patterned side down so that it stands on its tip, in the shape of a diamond. Then bring the bottom corner up over the top corner, folding in half to form a triangle.

2. Fold the left and right corners up diagonally so that they meet at the top corner and the edges lie along an imaginary centerline.

3. Turn the diamond thus created over, keeping the top corner at the top.

4. Fold the figure in half again, bringing the bottom corner up to the top corner to form a triangle.

5. Now fold the side points of this triangle up along a diagonal line that starts from the center of the lower edge; however, this time the diagonal fold should be at a steeper angle than in step 2. Here about ⅔ of each side is folded up and, by doing so, the layers of fabric are folded above one another. After the folding, the ends of the long tips should stick out above the napkin like little horns on the left and right left sides of the upper tip, and the side edges should line up with the creases.

6. The figure should look like drawing 6 at this point. Turn the napkin over once more.

7. At the top center point of the figure there are two tips of the very top layer of fabric that lie like two freely resting wings. Grab the wings at their upper tips and unfold each of them outward.

8. Now grab the second layer of fabric at the center tip and fold it forward and down.

9. The Jumping Frog is now complete and ready to decorate your table.

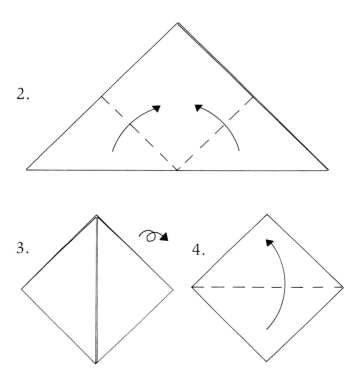

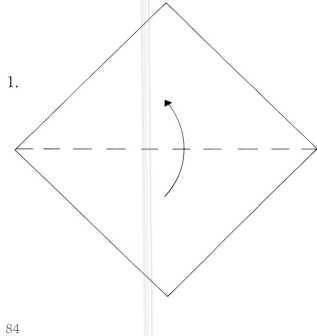

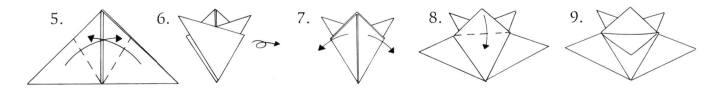

5. 6. 7. 8. 9.

Ice-Cream Cone

The tapered Ice-Cream Cone shows clearly how a few simple folds can produce an effective napkin form. Diagonally running edges, overlapping and offset, emphasize the austere contour of the figure and, at the same time, contibute to its dramatic appearance.

A plain cloth napkin allows these details to come out particularly well. If you choose napkins with a striped pattern to fold the Ice-Cream Cone, the fabric pattern highlights the diagonal offset lines to produce a striking and expressive result. With the plain variation, you can enhance the look of the design by using the deep pocket to hold a small flower, a favor for each guest, or simply their silverware, as we have done here.

Folding Instructions

1. Begin with a napkin folded into quarters; paper napkins come prefolded this way. To fold a napkin into quarters, fold the napkin in half, bringing the bottom edge up to the top edge to form a rectangle, and then fold in half left over right into a square. The loose four corners will be in the upper right.

Rotate the square to a diamond with the loose four corners at the left tip. The upper tip consists of two double-layered edges. Grab the one on top and fold it down to the lower tip.

2. Turn the napkin over, flipping the left corner to become the right as the top remains at the top.

3. Now fold the figure along a diagonal line starting from the lower tip for about one-third of the napkin toward the left.

4. The napkin should look like drawing 4. The left third is now folded on top of the already folded third, likewise starting in a diagonal line from the lower tip. Should the crease of the previous step turn out to be too narrow or too wide, you can still adjust it at this point. In any case, the folded thirds should lie precisely on top of one another, and the lower end of the napkin should taper to a point.

6. The right tip of the third that lies on top is now folded back and tucked in along the edge that runs diagonally below it. The Ice-Cream Cone is done.

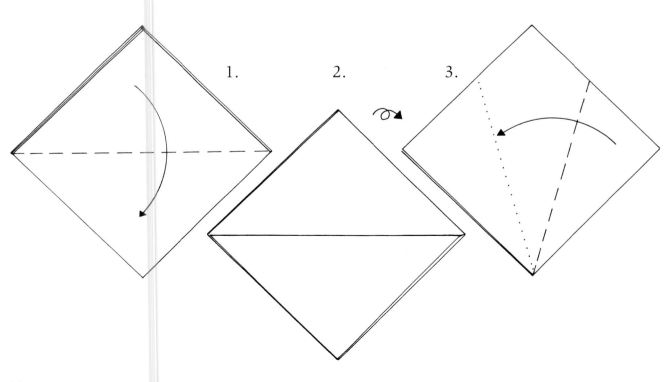

1.   2.   3.

4.

5.

6.

Contoured Fish

A true feast for the eyes, this napkin presents a striking decorative figure, the Contoured Fish. This is a stylish napkin shape not only for fish dishes, but for any occasion. When made with patterned paper, such as our wild tiger napkin, it can suggest an exotic fish with the ambiance of the tropics. This perfectly shaped napkin figure proves to be an attractive eye catcher, not only impressive but also very simple to create.

Its contours come about through a simple folding technique and a few tricks. Whether you prefer paper or cloth napkins for this figure is entirely up to you. Yet, if possible, use napkins that are no larger than 14 by 14 inches in order to avoid the fish becoming too large and flat.

Folding Instructions

1. Spread out the napkin face down on the table as a square in front of you. Fold the four corners inward to meet at the center.

2. This time fold three of the corners—the bottom, left, and right—once again inward to meet at the center.

3. Carefully turn your napkin over, keeping the point at the top.

4. Fold the two lower corners diagonally up to meet along an imaginary centerline of the napkin.

5. With the index finger of one hand, hold the tips of the corners just folded up, indicated with a circle on drawing 5. Now grab the flap that lies loose under the lower edge of the napkin and carefully pull it outward, as well as slightly up, so that it easily turns inside out. Reach again under the napkin and pull the left flap, which lies loose under the lower left end of the napkin, toward the outside. Do the same with the right corner, pulling the right flap out from behind.

6. Now place the finished Contoured Fish carefully on your plate.

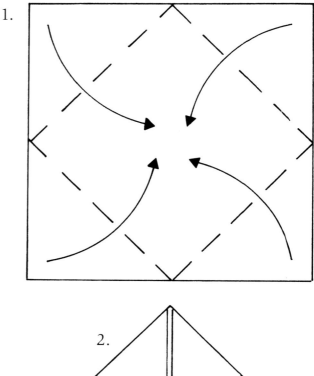

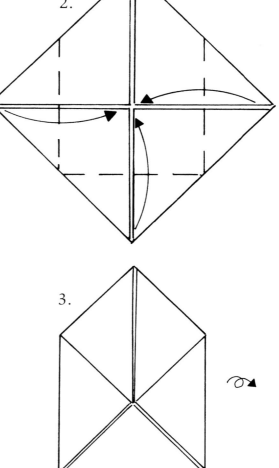

4.

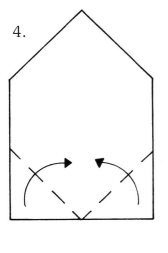

5.

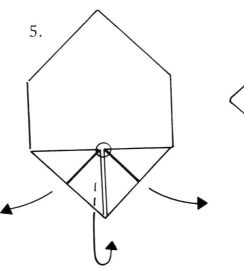

6.

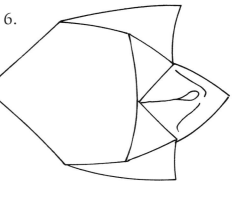

89

Arrowhead

If you want to show off the fine fabric or emphasize the expressive pattern of your napkins, a simple napkin form, such as this geometric Arrowhead, might be the perfect choice. The Arrowhead proves impressively that simple, in this case, does not mean plain but rather should be understood as an expression of noble elegance.

The sweeping effect of this attractive Arrowhead works very well for the dinner table with ordinary colored or patterned paper napkins. If you prefer cloth napkins, they should not be larger than 14 by 14 inches in order for your Arrowhead not to turn out too large and flat.

Folding Instructions

1. Spread the napkin with the right or patterned side down so that it stands on its tip, in the shape of a diamond. Then bring the top corner down over the bottom, folding in half to form a triangle.

2. Fold the the lower tip of the triangle up to the middle of the upper edge.

3. Fold the left and right sides of the napkin in half diagonally and inwards from the center of the upper edge; this is done in such a way that the former upper edges of the napkin come to rest along the upper edges of the triangle flap folded up in step 2.

4. Fold the creased sides again diagonally inward so that the former upper edges meet at at an imaginary centerline.

5. The only thing left for you to do is to turn the napkin over.

6. And here you have an Arrowhead that is perfectly shaped, ready to place artistically on your plate.

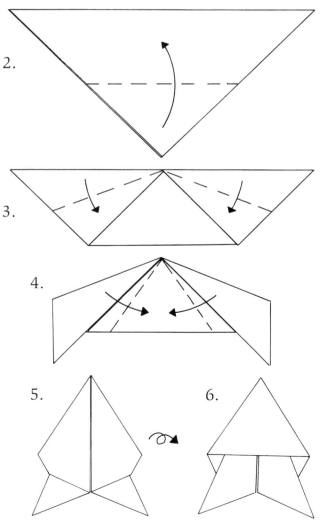

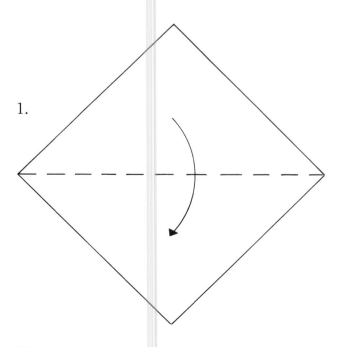

Prima Donna

To do justice to such a promising name that brings to mind grace and beauty, a very special napkin creation is called for—one that skillfully combines the finesse of the art of napkin folding, which is rich in tradition, with elegant simplicity. Now, you have to admit that our Prima Donna, created from airy layers of cloth, exceeds these expectations.

As to be expected, a Prima Donna makes certain demands. For her great appearance, you will need a cloth napkin 16 by 16 up to 18 by 18 inches in size, made of fine fabric if possible, such as damask, linen, or sheer batiste. The shapely Prima Donna has enough stability without starch; however, I do recommend that you use a little spray starch if you choose very soft fabrics. When you see how easily this artistic figure can be conjured up from a mere cloth napkin, the Prima Donna will certainly be part of your table decoration in the future.

Folding Instructions

1. Begin with the napkin spread out face down on the table in front of you so that it stands on its tip, in the shape of a diamond. Then bring the bottom corner over the top, folding the napkin up in half into a triangle.

2. Fold the left and right corners up diagonally so that they meet at the top corner and the edges lie along an imaginary centerline.

3. The napkin is now a smaller diamond shape. Fold the bottom half backward behind the top half, bringing the bottom tip up behind the top tip to form a triangle.

4. Grab the two loose wings, which rest freely above the napkin, by the tip and bring them up vertically.

5. With slight pressure onto the vertical folding edges, gently press down onto the lower edge of the napkin. Do not smooth the crease. With this procedure, the pointed wings open automatically, to become two small diamonds with inner points touching, as in drawing 6.

Since the small diamonds are supposed to turn into voluptuous folds in the next step, you are not allowed to smooth down the edges. Otherwise, these folds will not be able to fall softly or have the necessary integrity to support the finished napkin sufficiently.

6. The napkin should lie in front of you as shown in drawing 6, but the diamonds are not pressed flat. In this step, the two small diamonds are each gently folded horizontally in half and loosely folded up. It is also important that you do not smooth down the edges, so that the inner folds of the both double side folds remain slightly rounded, thus springing open softly.

7. Now you only need to loosely bend the two side tips of the napkin backward until they meet in the middle some distance behind.

8. In this way, the Prima Donna takes her shape automatically; the double side folds spring open and give the figure the necessary support.

1.

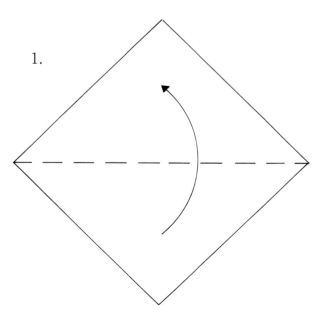

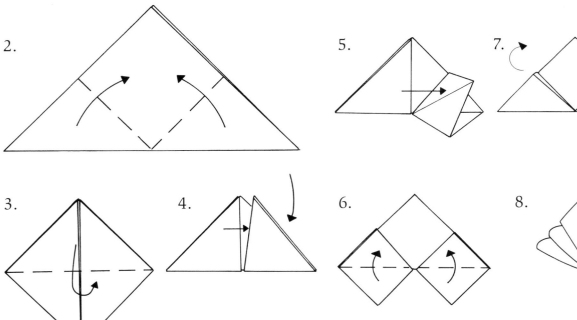

2.

3.

4.

5.

6.

7.

8.

Tucked Diamond

Who would expect this name, Tucked Diamond, to be such a charming beauty?

Yet an interestingly beautiful napkin creation lies hidden in this name, which has more to offer than the diamond shape—namely a striking appearance that comes by marrying strict, straight edges and soft, tucked layers of fabric.

For the square, simple 12 by 12 inches large napkins made of paper or fleece can be used, as with this figure neither the pre-embossed edges of the fold nor the back side disturb the appearance. If you prefer finer fabrics, you may certainly fold the square from fabric as well. Whichever variation you may decide on in the end, you should stay away, if possible, from any pattern. This interesting design has the greatest effect when made from a solid-colored material.

Folding Instructions

1. Spread out the napkin face down on the table as a square in front of you. Fold the four corners inward to meet at the center.

2. Fold the napkin backward in half diagonally so that the bottom right edge goes up around behind to meet the upper left edge. Turn the napkin clockwise so that top right edge becomes the bottom edge.

3. Now the rectangle should lie with the long side vertically in front of you, as in drawing 3. Fold the napkin down horizontally in half, bringing the top edge down to meet the bottom edge. Now rotate the napkin once more so that the lower right corner of the square becomes the upper tip of a diamond.

4. If the upper half of your napkin consists of four loose layers, the napkin is in the right position.

Now grab the free tip that lies on the very top of the half of the diamond. Fold this tip back and tuck it in, pushing it completely into the pocket-like opening until the edge of the fold is precisely running horizontally across the middle of the napkin.

5. Loosely fold the next upper tip forward, about two-thirds down, and tuck the end of this layer under the edge that runs horizontally across the diamond at the middle.

6. Then arrange the finished Tucked Diamond on your plate.

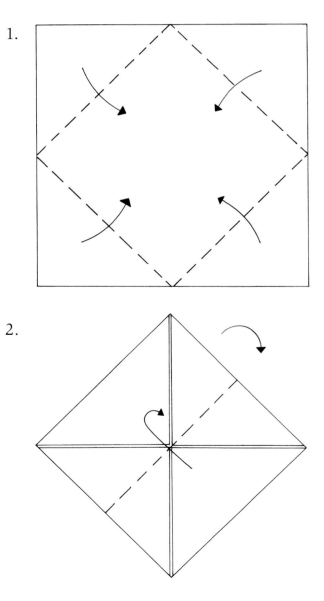

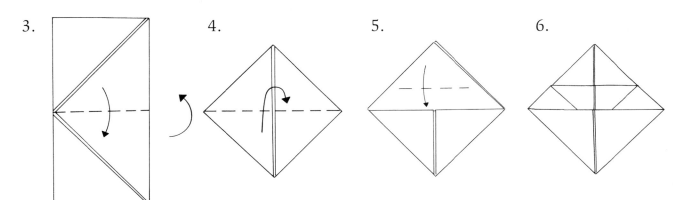

3. 4. 5. 6.

Roll with Point

The roll is a classic napkin form that catches our eye with its simplicity. This variation with the point accentuate luxurious lace edges, fine hemstitches, and timmings. It will also draw your guest's attention to monograms, pretty embroideries, and romance.

Napkins that have been stored folded will need to be smoothed or the earlier creases will disturb the clear appearance of the finished figure. Paper napkins do not work well not only because of the creases, but they are too thin and soft to hold the clean, firm look of the Roll with Point.

Folding Instructions

1. Spread out the napkin on the table in front of you so that it stands on its tip, in the shape of a diamond. But for this figure, the right or patterned side should be face up. Any embroidery or other design that you want to appear on the finished point should start visibly placed at the upper tip. Fold the bottom tip up, along a horizontal line one-third of the distance to the upper tip.

2. Then turn the napkin over, keeping the upper tip at the top.

3. On this side, the upper tip is folded down along a horizontal line that is the same distance below the upper tip as the crease for the fold in step 1 was above the lower tip. After folding, the former upper tip should end slightly above the lower edge.

4. Turn the napkin over once more, keeping the upper edge at the top.

5. Fold the two triangular outer edges inward, and then very loosely fold the two sides in by folding the figure in thirds, just as you would fold a letter, but do not press the creases.

6. Now slide the two sides that have been folded inward into each other at the upper edge. Again, don't smooth down these creases, but only tuck in the fabric! Keep in mind that the finished napkin figure should look like a soft roll.

7. Turn the napkin around so you can see the Roll with Point, and place it on your plate.

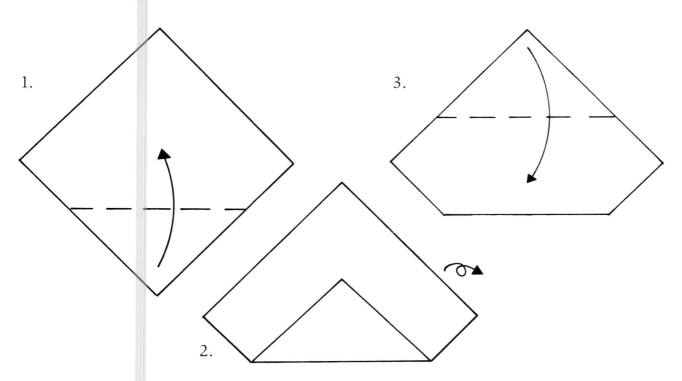

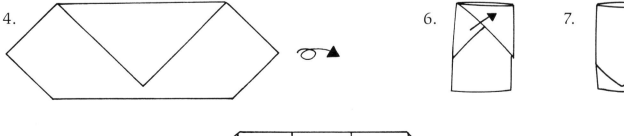

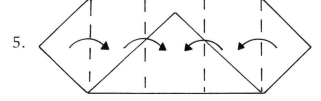

4.

5.

6.

7.

Winged Sibyl

Whether this form is made from plain cloth or from paper with a pretty pattern does not matter. Often it is precisely the simple napkin that radiate the most charm. Beyond that, such figures possess the wonderful advantage that they will turn out successfully without any difficulties. And so it is with the Winged Sibyl, which rests proudly and erect on wide wings.

Where its name originates, I cannot say. It likely comes from the name that is associated with several prophetesses of the ancient world. Our pretty Winged Sibyl will no doubt bring you good fortune on many occasions.

Folding Instructions

1. Spread out the napkin face down on the table. Fold in the middle, bringing the top edge down to the bottom edge to form a rectangle.

2. Bring the upper left and right corners diagonally down to meet at the center of the bottom edge.

3. The napkin lies now as a triangle in front of you. Fold the left and right corners diagonally up so that the corners meet on the upper tip.

4. The figure is now a diamond shape standing on its tip. Fold the diamond backward in half vertically, by bringing the right tip behind to meet the left tip.

5. Set up the napkin on its lower edge. The corners, which have been folded up in step 3, will fall open and will provide, if they are pulled slightly apart, the support for your Winged Sibyl to stand on the plate.

1.

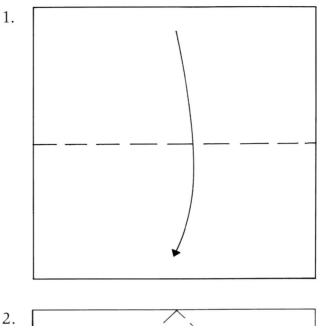

2.

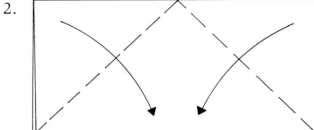

3.

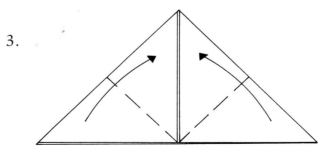

4.

5.

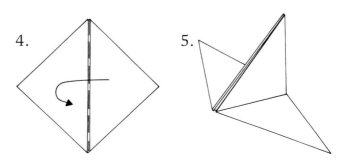

Ice Bird

As you might suppose from glancing at the clever folding technique, this exuberant Ice Bird actually does originate from origami, the Japanese art of paper folding. The Ice Bird is a stunning addition to the tradition of napkin folding and makes a lovely figure when worked in cloth. You may use any kind of napkin material in a standard size.

Folding Instructions

1. Spread out the napkin face down in the shape of a diamond on its tip. Fold the upper left and right edges of the napkin diagonally in to meet at an imaginary centerline.

2. Fold the lower tip up along the horizontal edges of the two flaps folded over in step 1. The lower flap folds up neatly as an isosceles triangle.

3. Now fold the lower third of the napkin up along a horizontal line.

4. Turn the napkin over, keeping the upper point at the top.

5. Fold about 2 inches of the upper tip down, and then fold back up about two-thirds of the folded tip.

6. The upper tip should look like drawing 6 without the arrows or dashed lines. Now grab the two side edges, right and left of the folded upper tip (at the upper arrows in drawing 6), and carefully press them together (folding along the dashed lines that the lower set of arrows point to). As you press the edges together, the folded tip will begin to stand up from the table surface.

7. Fold the protruded tip over toward the left so it lies flat on the napkin.

8. Bring the upper left corner back behind to meet the upper right corner, thus folding the napkin back in half along an imaginary centerline. After folding in half, place the figure on the folding surface so that it is flat on its side. The folded head should still be pointing to the left

9. Now grab the top layer at the lower right corner of the figure and fold it up diagonally so its bottom edge sits exactly on the front edge at the left.

10. Take the left edge of the flap just folded and bring it diagonally over to lie on its crease.

11. Now turn the napkin over.

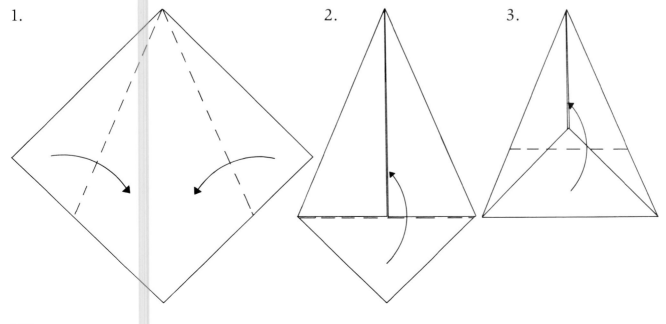

12. On this side, the bottom edge is again folded up diagonally to the front edge, now at the right. Then take the right edge of the flap just folded and bring it over diagonally to lie on its crease, which is now the back left edge of the Ice Bird.

13. Place the lower end of the finished Ice Bird into a narrow glass, allowing the figure to open slightly. You have created a stunning table decoration.

4.

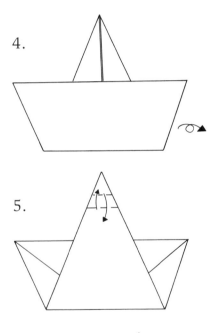

5.

6.

7.

8.

9.

10.

11.

12.

13.

Bat

This exotic napkin figure not only takes its name from its striking wings, but also from its overall appearance—the sweeping and expressive wings frame the fan-like opening folds in the center of the napkin, suggesting the ears above the body of the little Bat. Thus this figure is a true beauty that will not shy away from the limelight, contrary to its namesake.

You should use napkins from 12 by 12 to 16 by 16 inches in size. The front and back of the napkin are both visible with the finished Bat, so choose plain napkins or ones that are solid colored throughout. The folding of this figure, itself, gives the necessary support to stand on the plate with its large wings, so that you can use any napkin material to create a beautifully shaped Bat. If you find, however, that your napkins are too thin or too soft, I recommend a little spray starch for support.

Folding Instructions

1. Spread out the napkin in front of you as a square. Accordion-pleat the lower half of the napkin up to the middle, by folding a band about ⅝ to ¾ inch wide of narrow, zigzag folds starting from the lower edge. Smooth down the creases of the folds well. In the end, the folded part should run like a narrow band along the lower edge.

2. Fold the lower left and right corners diagonally up to meet at the center of the upper edge.

3. The figure is now an isosceles triangle with the tip facing you. Fold the lower tip of the triangle up along a horizontal line that is about one-third of the distance from the lower tip to the upper edge.

4. Grab the folded tip again and fold the flap down in half, bringing the tip to the lower edge.

5. Bring the upper right corner back behind to meet the upper left corner, thus folding the napkin back in half along an imaginary centerline. After folding in half, place the napkin figure flat on the folding surface.

6. The napkin should be lying on its side with the point at the upper left, as in drawing 6. Firmly press the lower end of the napkin to smooth down the creases at the bottom.

7. All you need to do is grasp the figure by its lower right edge, front and back, and place it upright on a plate. The pleated fans and folded wings will open automatically, balancing and supporting the figure of the Bat. You may want to smooth out the middle of each wing where there had been a fold.

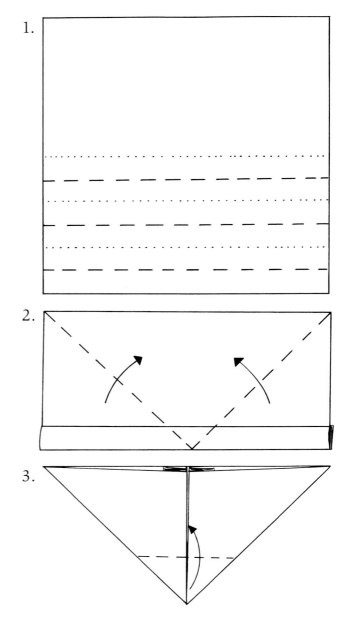

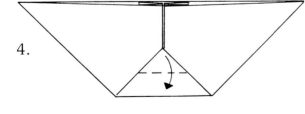

4.

5.

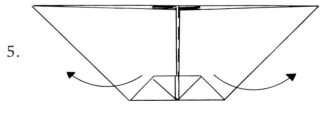

6.

7.

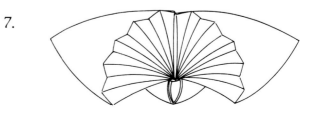

Castle

The name Castle, as well as the strict, upright form suggests that we are dealing here with a very old napkin figure that is rich in tradition.

However, as you can see, this imposing Castle has not lost any of its charm after all these years. Although this is not an elaborate form, but more of a minimalist creation, it should not be dismissed as a simple figure. It is precisely its extreme spareness and simplicity that gives it such striking elegance and timeless beauty. It is a purely realized form that should not be missing in your repertoire. For the Castle you may use any napkin material, cloth or paper, in any size you like. Trimmings or lace borders, in particular, are given a pretty accent with this figure.

Folding Instructions

1. Begin with the napkin spread out face down on the table in front of you so that it stands on its tip, in the shape of a diamond. Then bring the bottom corner over the top, folding the napkin up in half into a triangle.

2. Fold the left and right corners up diagonally so that they meet at the top corner and the edges lie along an imaginary centerline.

3. Fold the lower tip of the napkin up along a horizontal line that lies slightly below the center. The lower tip should comes to rest about 2 inches below the upper tip of the napkin.

4. Now gently bend the right and left corners of the napkin backward so they overlap, and then tuck the ends into one another.

5. And there you have your Castle, ready for you to arrange on your plate.

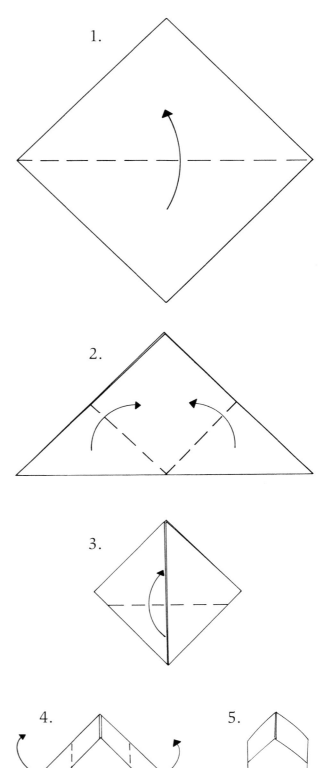

Dragonfly

In case you are still thinking that especially showy and intricate napkin figures must be complicated, difficult to fold and time consuming, then this pretty Dragonfly with its charming, delicate wings will certainly convince you of the opposite. With the exotically decorative Dragonfly, an impressive table can be conjured up in no time. In this case, it does not matter whether you have cloth napkins or colorful paper napkins at hand. No matter what, the result will fill you and your guests with enthusiasm.

The whole secret behind this striking figure is simply accordion pleating or fanning, by which the napkin is folded back and forth in narrow, sharp zigzag folds.

Folding Instructions

1. Spread the napkin with the right or patterned side down so that it stands on its tip, in the shape of a diamond. Then bring the top corner down over the bottom, folding in half to form a triangle.

2. Now begin, starting from the lower tip, to place the napkin into narrow accordion-pleat folds, about ¾ inch wide, simply by folding the napkin back and forth at a regular distance until it rests in front of you as a narrow band. According to your own preference, you may now more or less smooth down the creases of the folds. Clearly distinct edges can be very effective whereas rounded edges, subtle and barely visible, give a softer appearance.

3. If you were to let the napkin unfold slightly, it would look like drawing 3; however, the drawing is presented here merely to illustrate the principle of accordion pleating, or fanning. Your accordion-pleated napkin actually should be on the surface in front of you as a narrowly folded band, with the tip of the napkin at the middle and the edges running zigzag on both sides.

4. Your accordion-pleated napkin band should look like drawing 4. Now simply fold this band in the middle by folding the long sides together.

5. Without support, the Dragonfly cannot develop into its full beauty and, therefore, the folded middle has to be placed into a narrow glass. The slender wings then automatically open to their full size.

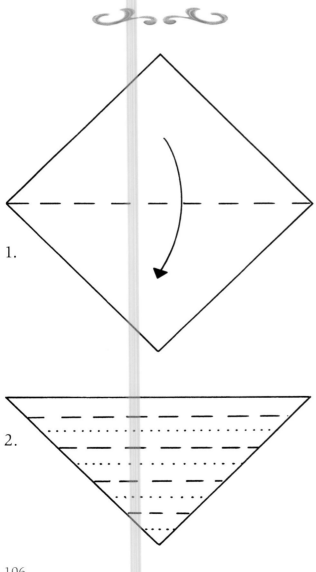

1.

2.

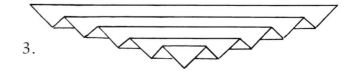

3.

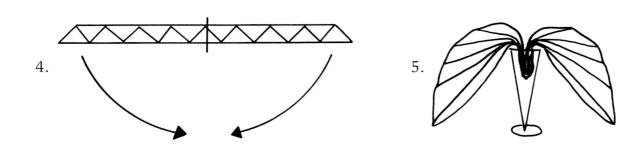

4.

5.

Medallion

If you would like a to show off a corner of lace, or bring some pretty embroidery into the limelight, then you should take a close look at this folding idea. This well-balanced napkin figure is called a Medallion because it encompasses the artistically embroidered corner of the napkin so elegantly and accentuates its perfected form.

Looking at its silhouette, the Medallion brings to mind the popular, but rather static, hat form. In this instance, however, the form appears much softer and pleasing. The rounded-off contours create—with finesse but, at the same time, unobtrusively—a nice frame for decorative napkin details.

The framing effect can be used not only for lace or embroidered napkins, but for skillfully presenting napkins with pretty designs, colorful borders, or bright trimmings as well. And, last but not least, simple paper napkins can be put into the spotlight in a lovely way with the Medallion.

Folding Instructions

1. Spread the napkin with the right or patterned side face down so that it stands on its tip, in the shape of a diamond. The corner ornamented with lace, a monogram, or embroidery is positioned under the lower tip of the napkin that points toward you. Now fold the left and right corners vertically inward so that the tips are facing one another at a distance of about 2 inches.

2. Fold the upper tip horizontally down for about one-third of the distance to the lower tip, as illustrated in drawing 2. The horizontal fold line should cross a small section of the corners, which had been folded toward the middle in step 1.

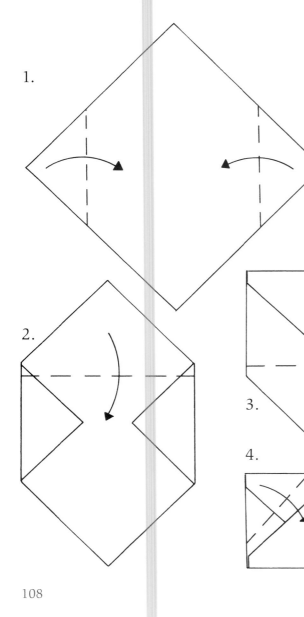

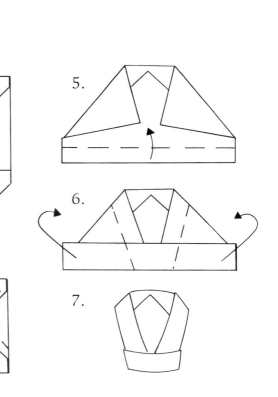

3. Fold the lower tip up likewise. The lower tip should come to rest slightly below the upper edge of the napkin.

4. Now fold the upper left and right corners of the napkin diagonally inward, as shown in drawing 4. The creases should be slightly to the outside of the visible tip so that they surround the tip.

5. Fold the lower edge horizontally up so that it just covers the two folded tips of step 4.

6. Now the only folding left to do is to bend back the left and right corners so that they overlap at the back of the napkin. Then tuck the corners into one another.

7. Finally, you will want to shape the finished Medallion as you arrange it on your plate. The inner side edges and the top edge that frame the inner tip should be gently rounded into an arch so that they form a continuous smooth frame surrounding the tip in a soft, curved line.

Airy Butterfly

Your family and guests will love this napkin figure. It brings an elated, cheerful touch of spring to any table decoration. And you only need some pretty paper napkins 12 by 12 inches or, even better, as large as 16 by 16 inches, to grace your table with these lovely creatures. Add some flowers to you Airy Butterflies and your table is transformed into a spring meadow. Naturally, you may also use cloth as the material of your choice; however, the fabric should not be too thick, for you want your creations to turn out nice and airy.

Folding Instructions

1. It is very important with this napkin figure that the right or patterned side of the napkin faces down at the beginning. Spread out the napkin face down as a square in front of you. Fold the napkin in half, bringing the top edge down to the bottom edge to form a rectangle.

2. At the lower edge, grab the layer of cloth lying on top and accordion-pleat it by folding the napkin back and forth at a width of about ⅜ to ⅝ inch into zigzag folds from the bottom up to the top edge.

3. Grab the napkin at the pleated upper corners, hold them tightly closed, and then turn the napkin over so the top edge beocmes the lower edge. The places at which to hold the napkin are marked with small circles in drawing 3.

4. The narrow, folded portion of the napkin should now lie below the lower edge of the napkin. Hold the center of the lower edge with one finger and then fold the lower left and right corners diagonally up meet at the center of the upper edge.

5. Grab the napkin in the middle of the upper edge and hold the two pleated ends tightly closed. Then turn the napkin over, by flipping the top edge to become the bottom edge.

6. Now fold the left and right corners diagonally up, starting from the center the lower edge, bringing them to meet at the upper tip. Then slide the tips into the small pocket-like layer of cloth at the tip.

7. Fold the entire napkin down horizontally in half, bringing the upper tip down to lie on the lower tip.

8. Grab the tip that was just folded down and fold it up again, creasing it a little above halfway; in other words, just so far up that the tip reaches slightly beyond the upper edge of the napkin.

9. Fold the left and right tips of the napkin inward, overlapping them, and then tuck the ends into one another.

10. Now all you need to do is turn the napkin over onto its front side.

11. By doing so, the wings unfold automatically. If you like, you can shape the body slightly rounder and narrower by squeezing it a bit before you place your Airy Butterfly on your plate.

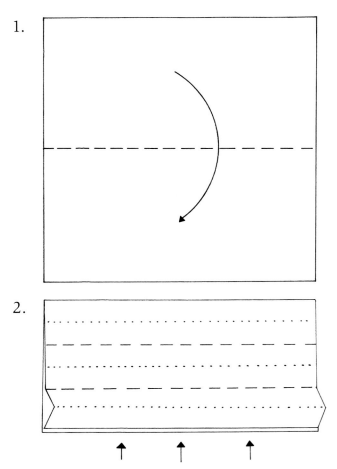

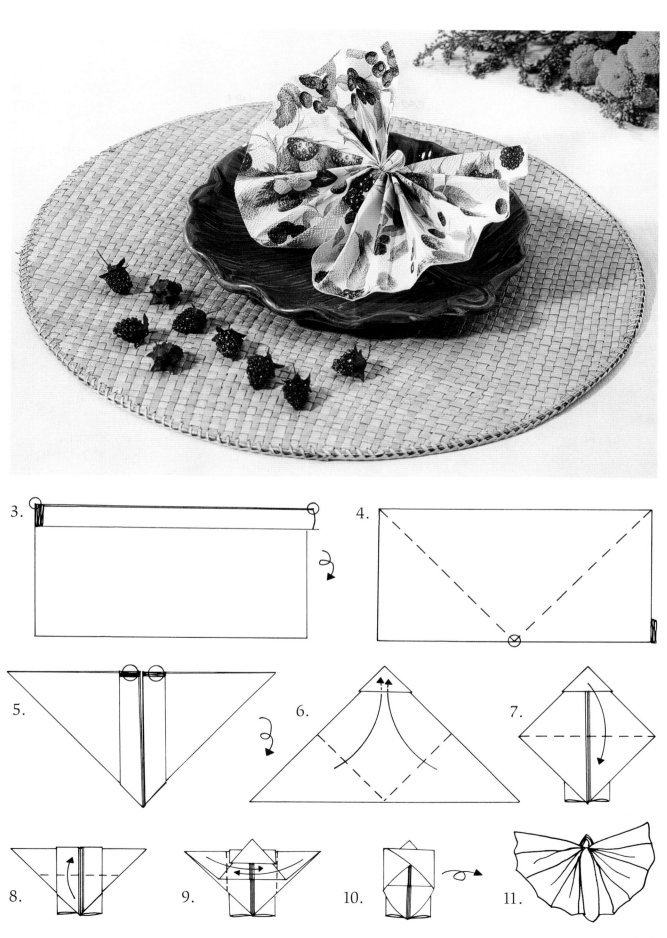

3.

4.

5.

6.

7.

8.

9.

10.

11.

Pelican

This expressive Pelican stylistically captures the bird perfectly in its sublime posture. With nobly spread wings and a distinct bill, this proud bird will impress your guests when they discover your whimsical table decoration.

It is important that you use firm, even possibly slightly starched, cloth napkins from 16 by 16 up to 18 by 18 inches in size, in order to give the Pelican its necessary stability. Tucking aluminum foil in between the layers of cloth for strength is a little trick from restaurateurs and hoteliers; however, this trick is only recommended if you are going to use the Pelican for decoration as a centerpiece or on a buffet table.

Folding Instructions

1. Spread out the napkin with the right side face down in the shape of a diamond on its tip. Fold the upper left and right edges of the napkin diagonally in to meet at an imaginary centerline.

2. Fold the lower tip back behind the napkin, with the crease running horizontally from the left corner to the right corner.

3. Fold the left and right edges of the triangle, just created in step 2, once more diagonally inward to meet at the center.

4. Before folding the napkin horizontally a little more than in half, look carefully behind to see where there is a tip positioned on the back side. Now fold slightly more than in half by bringing the upper tip down, but make sure this crease still runs above the tip on the back side. The tip folded down should wind up extending about ¾ inch beyond the edge of the napkin.

5. Fold the bottom tip that extends beyond the edge of the napkin up once more so that it comes to lie just below the upper edge.

6. The entire napkin is then folded backward in half along an imaginary vertical centerline.

7. Now set the napkin down on its long outer edges. Gently pull these edges apart at the rear open end to give the the Pelican steady support. The only thing left for you to do is to slightly pull the head and neck up and also outward.

8. Your jaunty Pelican is completed and ready to take up residence, sitting smartly on your plate.

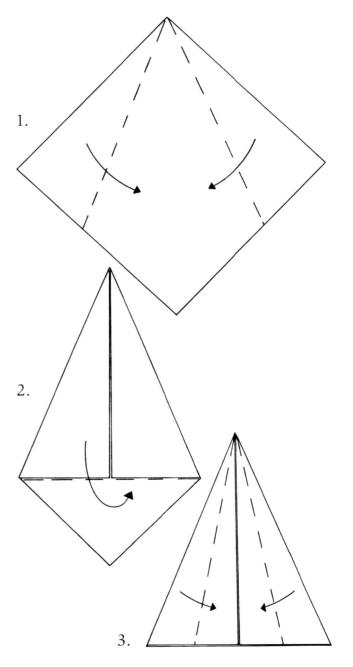

4.

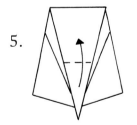

5.

6.

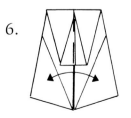

7.

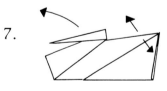

8.

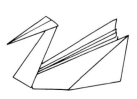

Bull's Head

Airy butterflies, graceful birds, or even exotic fish are again and again popular models for decorative folding figures. However, this imposing Bull's Head shows that the art of napkin folding is not limited to diminutive creatures but can take on large animals as well.

This napkin form, with its distinctive jutting horns, is reminiscent of the longhorns, the cattle of the southwest United States with impressive horns that are particularly appreciated for their delicious beef. When a figure is so perfectly stylized, it calls for associations to its suggested culinary pleasures. Why not present this splendid Bull's Head at your next barbecue or steak dinner?

Choose napkins at least 16 by 16 inches in size so the Bull's Head does not to turn out too small. If available, use napkins made of cotton or coarse linen to underline the rustic touch.

Folding Instructions
1. Spread the napkin with the right side face down so that it stands on its tip, in the shape of a diamond. Then bring the top corner over the bottom, folding the napkin down in half into a triangle.

2. Fold the sides of the triangle, starting from the middle of the top edge, diagonally inward so that the former top edges meet at the center above an imaginary centerline.

3. The napkin is now a smaller diamond shape. Fold the upper half backward behind the bottom half, bringing the upper tip down behind the bottom tip to form a triangle.

4. Fold the left and right tips diagonally backward along lines that start slightly away from the middle of the top edge, as shown in drawing 4.

5. The only thing left for you to do is to individually grab the two narrow tips, which rest as the layer of cloth at the very top on the lower tip. Then carefully pull them up and also outward, until, as they turn slightly inside out, they jut out like horns above the napkin.

During these two actions of pulling out the horns, I recommend that you use your free hand to hold the rest of the napkin together, squeezing the head so that the previous folds do not inadvertently come undone.

6. You can now place the finished Bull's Head on your plate.

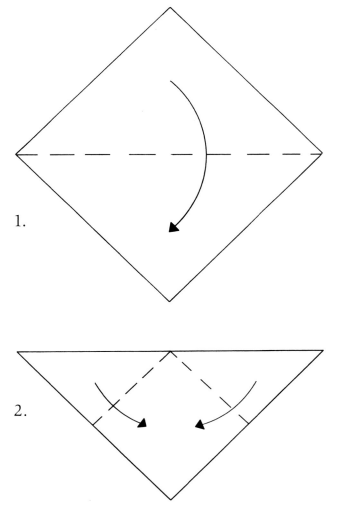

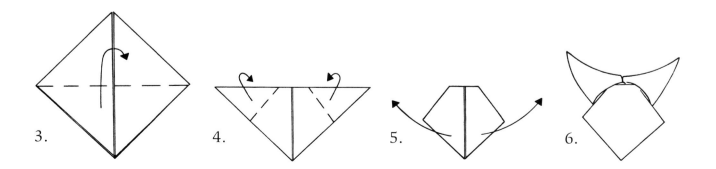

3. 4. 5. 6.

Dinner Jacket

Perhaps a formal dinner or a great festivity is going to take place. As an elegant Dinner Jacket dressed in flawless white and true to style with black bowtie, a simple napkin can bring just the right touch of class to a festive occasion. The elegant appearance of the Dinner Jacket takes little effort to make, yet it will add just the right festive touch to your table and will certainly delight your guests.

For a really stylish Dinner Jacket, only a cloth napkin made of fine material such as damask, linen, or batiste is suitable. Your choice of napkin size is really up to you since, in final folding step, you can vary the width and height of your Dinner Jacket by adjusting the width of the folds.

Folding Instructions

1. Spread out the napkin face down on the table in the shape of a diamond. Fold the napkin up in half, bringing the bottom corner to the top corner.

2. Fold up the bottom edge of the triangle forming a strip approximately ¾ to 1¼ inches wide.

3. Turn the napkin over, flipping the upper point down to become the lower tip that now is pointing toward you. The narrow folded band should be behind the upper edge.

4. Now simply fold the sides of the triangle forward and down; that is, each one is folded slightly away from the center of the upper edge. You can adjust the distance between the folds for the neck width.

5. The napkin should look as shown in drawing 5. For the completion of the Dinner Jacket, all you need to do is to simply fold the two sides and the lower tip backward.

6. The Dinner Jacket can now be given the final touch by placing a small tuxedo tie made of black silk on it.

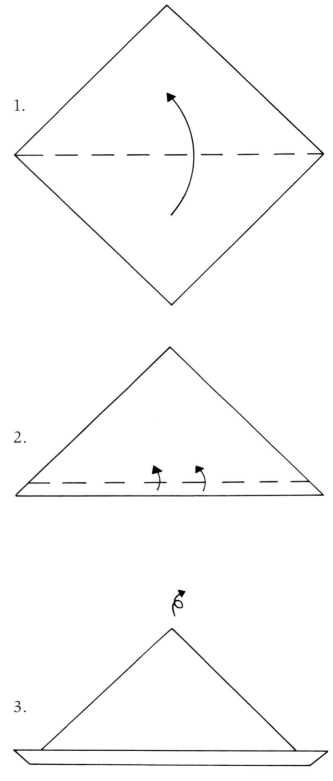

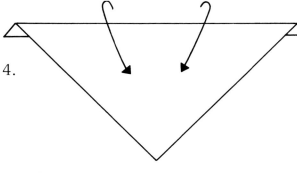
4.

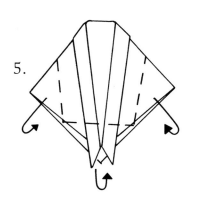
5.

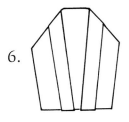
6.

117

French Fan

Fan-like napkin forms have been among the most popular decorative elements of a festive table for a very long time. This is not without reason, for whether strictly pleated or gathered up in soft folds, with its tips elegantly fanned open and soaring, these fans give each table decoration a special touch.

This figure is a classic example—the French Fan. Although the French Fan may look complicated and time-consuming, it is nevertheless quite easy to make. Even from simple paper napkins, impressive fans can be conjured up. The front and back of your napkin will be visible, so the napkin should have a pattern or color on both sides, and be 12 by 12 to 16 by 16 inches in size.

Folding Instructions

1. Spread out the napkin with the right side face down as a square in front of you. Fold the upper left and right corners diagonally inward, starting from the center of the upper edge, to meet at the middle of the napkin.

2. Grab the tips of the folded corners, and fold them diagonally outward so that the tips slightly jut out beyond the upper edges of the napkin.

3. The upper part of your folded napkin should now look as shown in drawing 3. Fold the lower part of the napkin up horizontally in half until the lower edge runs across the middle of the napkin.

4. Grab the left and right tips of the flap just folded up and bring them diagonally down, folding along lines starting from the center of the napkin edge going to the lower left and right corners.

5. The folded napkin should look like drawing 5. Fold the lower half of the napkin horizontally up, so far that the edge of the napkin runs just above the base of the folded corners that are springing open.

6. The napkin is now placed into approximately five large folds by folding it back and forth. The folds, whose creases point up, should run through the tips of the napkin. To make things easier, start with the crease through the tip in the middle and then place the sides each into two large folds.

7. As the charm of this fan lies in the lovely folds, which are softly gathered up and which will fall open, you do not want to smooth down the creases too severely, if at all. It is enough to simply hold the fan firmly together at the lower edge and to put this end into a glass or a napkin holder. The French Fan will then develop its splendor all by itself.

Tip: This many-sided napkin creation has a charming and very impressive effect when observed from all directions. Try out various placements to find which appearance suits your table decoration best!

1.

2.

3.

4.

5.

6.

7.

Greek Cross

As a stunning example of a napkin that perfectly matches the occasion, I do not wish to keep this Greek Cross, perfect in its form, from you.

It is perfectly suited for large or small family celebrations of personal and communal spiritual importance, whether it is Easter dinner a baptism, communion, confirmation, or wedding.

A perfect contrast to the strict form of the Greek Cross can be reached by using napkins with woven borders or complicated lace trimmings.

In order to have such a striking Greek Cross emerge in its elegant simplicity from a plain napkin, a few clever, but by no means difficult, folding steps are necessary.

Folding Instructions

1. Spread out the napkin with the right side face down on the table as a square in front of you. Fold the four corners inward to meet at the center. Smooth down the creases well after each fold.

2. Carefully turn the napkin over.

3. Again fold all four corners inward to meet at the center.

4. The napkin should now lie in front of you as shown in drawing 4. Turn the folded napkin over once more.

5. For the third time, fold all four corners inward to meet at the center.

6. And once again, turn the napkin over.

7. Now reach from the side into the open tips that rest freely on the center of the napkin so that you hold only one layer of cloth in your fingers. Then carefully pull these tips outward one by one. In this way, the small diamonds that lie on the napkin will open up on the sides and flatten to become the small rectangles, with the corners of the napkin lying below them.

8. Now all that is left to do is to smooth down the rectangles, which give the napkin its form of the cross. You can arrange the finished Greek Cross on your plate.

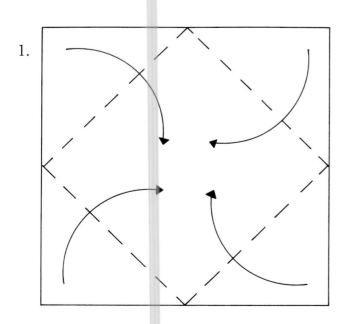

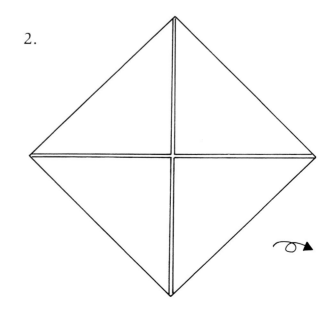

3.

4.

5.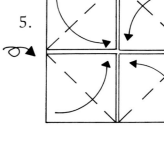

6.

7.

8.

Oyster

This splendid Oyster will be the eye-catching detail of your exquisite dinner decoration that will, without a doubt, impress your guests. This is a very time-consuming figure and certainly not a napkin form for everyday use. It is ideal, however, for those really special occasions as the highlight for festive tables. Follow attentively through the steps, using a fine napkin at least 16 by 16 inches in size, and you will brilliantly master the elegant Oyster.

Folding Instructions

1. Spread out the napkin face down in front of you as a square. Thus, the right or patterned side should be underneath. Now fold the upper fourth of the napkin down and the lower fourth up horizontally so that the top and bottom edges meet at the center.

2. Turn the napkin over, keeping the upper edge at the top.

3. Now fold the napkin lengthwise in half, bringing the right edge over to lie on the left edge.

4. First, place your finger on the center of the upper edge, at the upper M in drawing 4. Then grab the top free corner A and fold it toward the right onto corner B. The napkin will open up automatically into a wide, pointed cone. Then, fold on the dashed

lines. After you smooth down the creases, the folded part of the napkin should lie like a flat triangle on the upper half of the napkin. The left edge of the lower half that was below corner A stays at the left edge.

5. Following this, the right side of the flat triangle is once again folded back toward the left by grabbing once more tip A and folding it back to the left edge. During this folding, the left upper quarter of the napkin keeps the slanted creases.

6. The folding procedure described in steps 4 and 5 is now repeated in a mirror-like fashion on the lower half of the napkin.

7. The napkin should now lie in front of you as depicted in drawing 7, with two double-fold edges that run diagonally from the center of the upper and lower edge to the middle of the left edge. The next thing is to turn the napkin over, flipping it toward you, so the top edge becomes the bottom edge and the left edge remains at the left.

8. Steps 4 to 6 are also repeated on this side of the napkin so that there is now an upper and lower left edge at a slant toward one tip at the left.

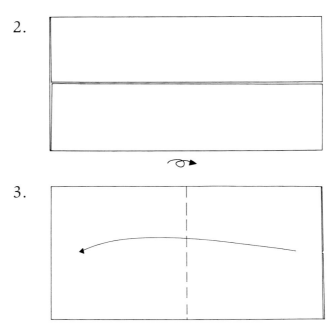

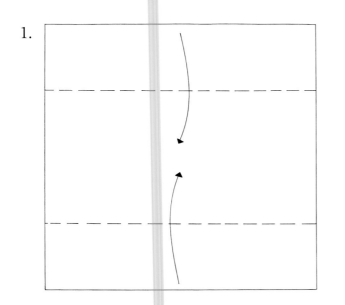

9. In this step, first place your finger on the middle of the right edge. Then reach on the lower edge in between the two layers of fabric and grasp corner C, which lies on the very top. Now bring corner C up to lie on corner D by folding the layer of cloth, which lies on the very top, horizontally up in half. In this way, the napkin opens automatically from the lower right corner into a wide cone, which you then smooth down.

10. After smoothing down, the cone then lies as a flat triangle above the right half of the napkin. Now turn the napkin over, flipping the top edge down to become the bottom edge.

11. Now proceed on this side just as described in step 9: fold the lower tip C up to point D. Smooth down the creased right half of the napkin into a flat triangle. The figure now has a diamond shape.

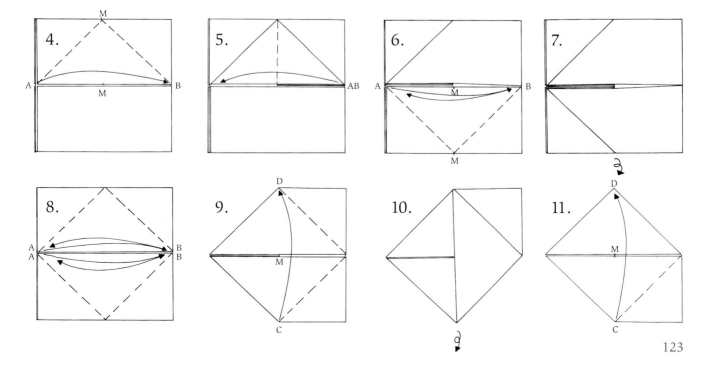

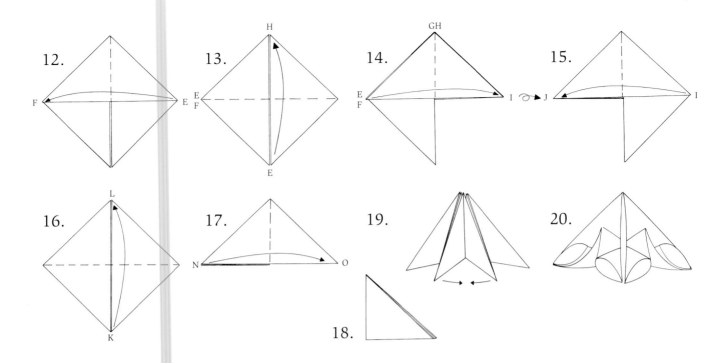

12. Now turn the napkin in front of you so that the tips, which are divided in its half, point down. Then fold the upper of the two right corner layers, at E, toward the left onto corner F.

13. Now fold the corner G, that is, the upper two free tips, up onto point H, by folding up the two layers of cloth lying on top in half horizontally.

14. Your folded napkin should now look as shown in drawing 14. The very top left corner E of the napkin is now folded towards the right onto corner I. Now turn the napkin over, left to right, by flipping the left corner over to become the right corner. The upper point stays at the top.

15. Now reach, from the right side, in between the two layers of cloth, and fold the layer of cloth, which lies on the very top of the right half of the napkin, toward the left, bringing corner I over to lie on corner J.

16. Fold the lower half of the entire folded napkin horizontally up to form a triangle. That is, all of corners K comes up onto L.

17. Fold this triangle in half from left to right, bringing all of corner N over onto corner O.

18. The many-layered small triangle, which has been created through these folding steps, is now set up on the bottom edge with the lower points facing you. Now pull two tips on either side outward and open them toward the back until they are facing each other at an obtuse angle. This should allow the napkin to be sufficiently stable to stand.

19. The two inner points are then pushed back together toward the middle.

20. Within each of the four double-layered points are free tips, the corners of which point up. First, grab these tips and roll each pair of tips into a cone shape toward one another.

Now shape the inner points as they are pushed down by rolling the pairs of tips. These inner points are also pulled forward and reduced in height by the rolled pairs of tips to complete this distinctive form of the Oyster.

Now that you have mastered this intricate form, you are ready to fold a set for your festive dinner.

Illustrated Index

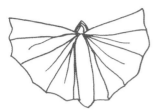

Airy Butterfly, 110

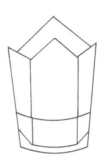

Bishop's Miter, 26

Castle, 104

Angel, 76

Bow Tie, 54

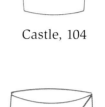

Chapeau, 80

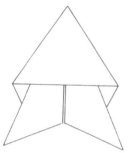

Arrowhead, 90

Bud, 32

Christmas Tree, 66

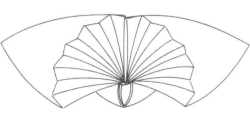

Bat, 102

Bull's Head, 114

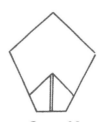

Cone, 20

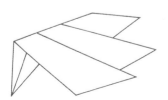

Bent Leaf, 62

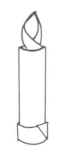

Candle, 64

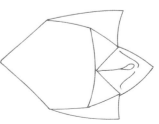

Contoured Fish, 88

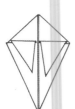

Cornucopia, 58

Dragonfly, 106

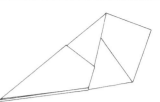

Ice-Cream Cone, 86

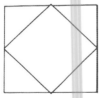

Diagonal Band, 30

Elegant Flower. 12

Jabot, 70

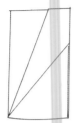

Diagonal Fold, 31

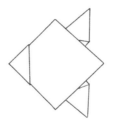

French Fan, 118

Jumping Frog, 84

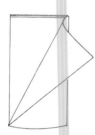

Diamond in the Square, 60

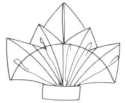

Funny Fish, 42

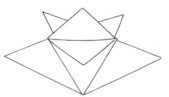

Lady's Slipper, 74

Dinner Jacket, 116

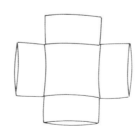

Greek Cross, 120

Little Horn, 50

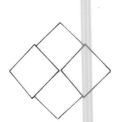

Double Diamond, 72

Ice Bird, 100

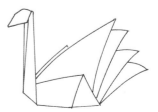

Little Swan, 34

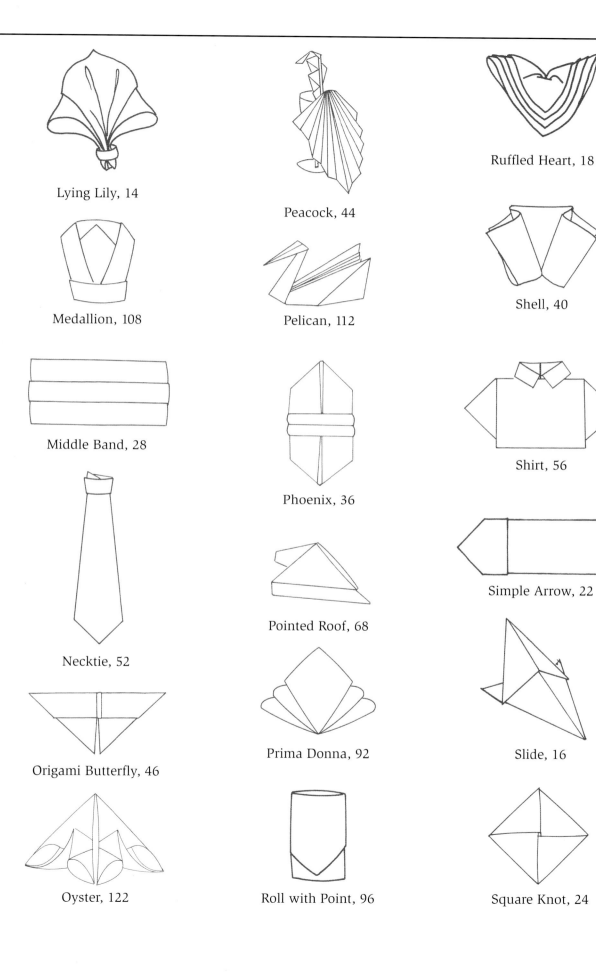

Lying Lily, 14

Peacock, 44

Ruffled Heart, 18

Medallion, 108

Pelican, 112

Shell, 40

Middle Band, 28

Phoenix, 36

Shirt, 56

Necktie, 52

Pointed Roof, 68

Simple Arrow, 22

Origami Butterfly, 46

Prima Donna, 92

Slide, 16

Oyster, 122

Roll with Point, 96

Square Knot, 24

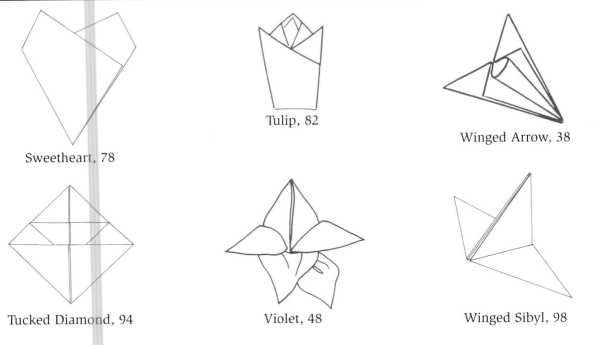

Sweetheart, 78

Tulip, 82

Winged Arrow, 38

Tucked Diamond, 94

Violet, 48

Winged Sibyl, 98

Metric Equivalents

[to the nearest mm, 0.1cm, or 0.01m]								

inches	mm	cm	inches	mm	cm	inches	mm	cm
⅛	3	0.3	2½	64	6.4	13	330	33.0
¼	6	0.6	3	76	7.6	14	356	35.6
⅜	10	1.0	3½	89	8.9	15	381	38.1
½	13	1.3	4	102	10.2	16	406	40.6
⅝	16	1.6	5	127	12.7	17	432	43.2
¾	19	1.9	6	152	15.2	18	457	45.7
⅞	22	2.2	7	178	17.8	19	483	48.3
1	25	2.5	8	203	20.3	20	508	50.8
1¼	32	3.2	9	229	22.9	21	533	53.3
1½	38	3.8	10	254	25.4	22	559	55.9
1¾	44	4.4	11	279	27.9	23	584	58.4
2	51	5.1	12	305	30.5	24	610	61.0

Conversion Factors

1 mm	=	0.039 inch	1 inch	=	25.4 mm	mm	=	millimeter
1 m	=	3.28 feet	1 foot	=	304.8 mm	cm	=	centimeter
						m	=	meter